Introduction

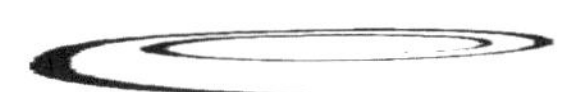

Life is full of anticipation, happiness and love. The secret is to find these ingrediences, balance them and stroll through life surrounded by harmony and the wonderment of God's creations. My joy is sharing the gift of imagination with others.

During the last year my path changed. I have been and seen places I once dreamt about. I am sure my husband never envisaged how wide spread his dream would become. Where ever I go I can take my dreams and craft with me. There are changing seasons, climates and soils and with these come a never ending variety of flowers. The anticipation of what flower will bloom next, the happiness in finding it and the love of imitating it with craft punches and paper, gives me inner harmony and I never cease to wonder.

An ivitation, from an American business associate, to demonstrate and talk to people concerning Floral Punch Craft was very exciting. A wonderful friendship began and from this, I have been given the opportunity to design craft punches. My latest designs will be released in conjunction with the launch of this book, Floral Punch Craft V. The petals and leaves for the Lilac, Iris, Daphne and Iris displays in this book were cut freehand. There are two punches, each capable of punching the shapes for two different flowers. One side for one flower, the other side for a different flower. Flowers, vases and baskets, this is indeed dreamland.

In Floral Punch Craft IV, I outlined a variety of shapes formed with the first punch I designed, Leone's Tree. In this book, the Horseshoe has many designs. There are three new character shapings, Rolling, Pendulum and Wave. When you read the Character Chart, you will understand and realise how easy each mouding is.

The sub title for the book is Versatility. The more I work with craft punches, the more I design. The new character shaping "Rolling" is achieved with the closed tweezers. Those with a Quilling tool, have a choice of the tweezers or the tool. Simple Heat Embossing, Paper Embossing and Stencilling along with the use of copper and aluminium illustrate why Floral Punch Craft is so versatile. I have been using these techniques for years and thought you might like to join in and enjoy these various combinations. Included is Cake Decorating and a beautiful little brooch with the appearance of porcelain. For the first time, I have given instructions for the same flower in 3D and flat. The flat designs include the layouts for Scrapbooking.

Floral Punch Craft is not an expensive craft. I started with one punch and numerous items around the house, meat skewer, ball point pen and a knitting needle that I still use. A few punches will get you started. If you have a similar punch to the one recommended, use it. Punched shapes are trimmed to create other shapes.

To new readers, welcome to the magical world of Floral Punch Craft. Many new punches are now available. Punches are an investment that will open up a new dimension of happiness for yourself and the new friends you will make in your quest for personal enjoyment.

Day by day, the world grows smaller.

Communication around the world
grows and blooms
through the friendships
formed in Floral Punch Craft.
We reach the mystical land
over the rainbow
through the doorway of colour
and imagination.
Take from this craft
the shared happiness
and
sense of achievement it brings.

Published January, 2002 by
Em Designs,
P.O. Box 34,
Rosanna, Victoria, 3084.
Australia.

Phone No. 61 3 9459 3802

e-mail
leone@floralpunchcraft
WebSite
www.floralpunchcraft.com

Designed and illustrated by Leone Em.

Printed in Australia by Impact Printing.

National Library of Australia
Cataloguing-in-Publication data:

Docherty, Leone M
Floral Punch Craft V.

ISBN 0957785739

DISCLAIMER
The information in this book is presented in good faith. However no warranty is given, nor results guaranteed, nor is the freedom from patent inferred.

Contents

Character Chart.

Character is the word used to change the shape of the paper. It can be used in conjunction with moulding or on its own. Character brings the shape to life.

Etching the veins into a leaf is giving the leaf character.

Turning petals / leaves inwards or outwards is giving character.

Shaping a stem or part of a petal is giving character.

Character is also painting or tinting to copy nature.

Half moon: Can be Horizontal.

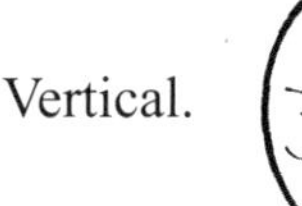

Vertical.

Up Side Down when glued.

Beehive: Is up-side-down cup shaping.

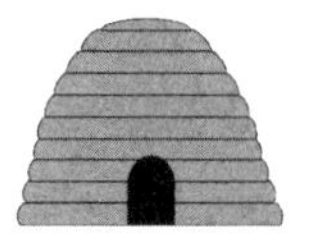

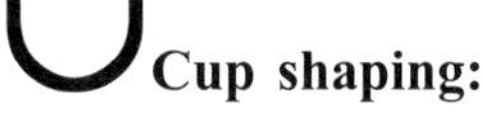

Cup shaping:

Cup shaping can be severe or mild.

Curling:

For Curling the edges of petals.

Wrap around shaping:
Wrap around character is described in full, with diagrams, on Page 7. Sometimes, the result after gluing will be a cone shape for a calyx.

Pendulum:

The tool moves like the clock's pendulum.

Collar:

A collar is glued around the pointed base of a completed flower. This allows the flower to stand upright. It also adds height to a flower in a floral arrangement.

The collar, diagram above and the wedge below, are made from a strip of matching paper.

Wave:

Combination of moulding both sides of the shape.

Wedge:
This is placed underneath the flower when gluing a shape on an angle.

Conversion ruler in inches, centimetres and millimetres.

Character Shaping Instruction.

Veining Character:
The length of DEET'S needle is used for **"character veining"**, not the point of the needle. Place the leaf on the moulding pad. Hold the tool flat/horizontal on the leaf. The palm of your hand must be above the tool.

NOTE: Flat/horizontal means flat like the horizon or workbench/table. See diagram below.

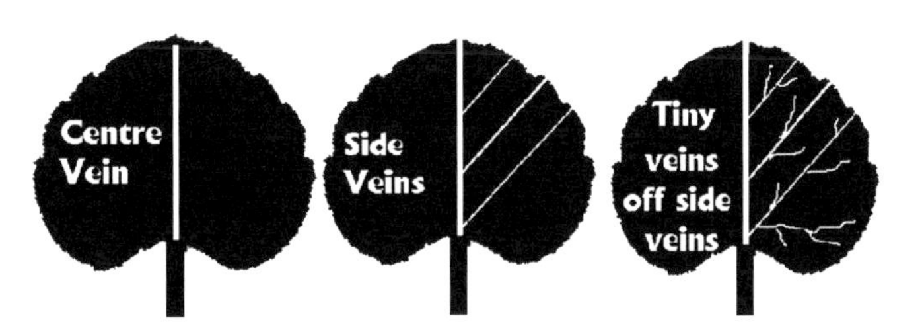

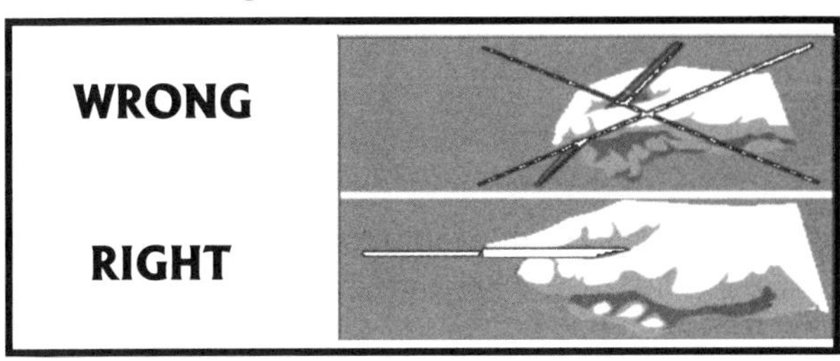

Centre vein: Slide DEET with downwards pressure, firmly along the length, in the centre of the leaf shape and onto the pad.
Side veins: Repeat the action commencing from the centre vein outwards onto the pad.

Hand Curving Character:
Character can be given to petals, stems, leaves and ribbons by holding the base of the shape between the thumb and index finger of your left hand. With the etching tool in your right hand, place the needle end behind the shape, at the position where you want the shaping to commence. With your right thumb pressing the shape onto the needle, pull the tool upwards and away from your body and you obtain a simple backwards curve. The more pressure on the needle with the thumb of your right hand the more curving is achieved. By placing the needle in front of the shape and pulling the tool towards your body, the curve will come forward. For a left handed person, reverse the instructions. A petal can have a little of both methods when extra life-like character is needed. Angle the tool and you achieve a sideways curve.

Painting and/or Tinting Character:

Combine with water and paintbrush

Water soluble pencils

water soluble crayons

or paints.

Wet surface:
With the paintbrush, dampen the shape with water before applying the colour. The colour will run giving a dappled effect. When two colours are applied to a wet shape, they will bleed together. Use pink and yellow to try this method.
Dry surface:
When the colour is applied to a dry surface, the coloured character lines and splashes are more definite. These can be softened, if necessary, with the paintbrush and a little water.

Paintbrushes:
A large shape requires a No. 4 paintbrush, very small a No. 0 and/or a Liner brush for character lines.

Palettes:
Make two palettes from a cheap plastic cutting board with a slightly rough surface.
Cut the board in half and use both sides. Rub the lead, side on, of the water soluble pencil or the end of a crayon onto the boards. Leave the colours on the boards after painting. Add water via the paintbrush, when required. Several colours can be blended together to acquire various shades. Use one side for greens and earthy colours while the other side has purples and reds. The colour combination is up to the individual. Black is a valuable shade to include. A touch of black to red gives you a dusty pink shade.

Rolling: Rolling is Quilling with the closed tweezers taking the place of the Quilling tool. Rolling becomes a tight coil when completed. Remove the tweezers, after adhering the end of the paper to secure the coil.
To add another length of paper to the completed coil, place one arm of the tweezers into the centre of the coil and, the other on the outside. Adhere the end, roll, secure the end and remove from the tweezers.
Note: There is variation between individuals when rolling with the closed tweezers/quilling tool, and also, the type of paper used. Spare petals are to fill in any gaps that appear after rolling is completed.

Character Shaping Instructions *continued:*

Half Moon Character:

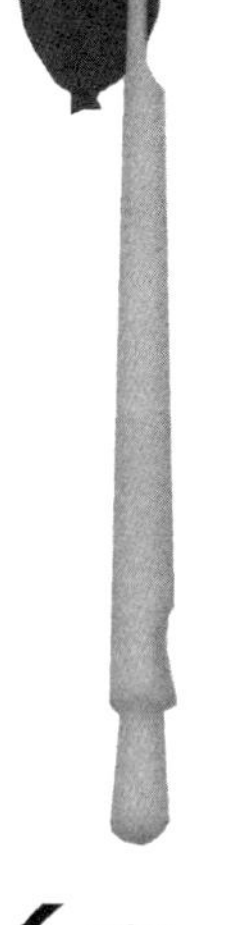

Place the shape on the edge of the moulding pad. Hold the white moulding tool horizontal. This requires the palm of your hand to be over the top of the tool.
Turn the small half round end of the white tool onto its knife edge with the rounded side facing the direction in which you will move your hand.

Example: A right handed person will move the hand holding the tool, from right to left, this requires the curved side to be facing left.

Use the knife edge of the tool and slowly stroke across the shape from right to left (opposite for left handed individuals) similar to spreading butter on bread, use a little downwards pressure. The shape will curve giving **"half moon character".** For **"severe half moon"** shaping move the tool across the shape several times with more pressure on the tool each time.
"Half moon character" is usually across the width of a petal or a leaf. When you become used to creating this shape, you will gain speed.

Cup Character: 

Size. Use the tool most suitable for the shape. Large shapes require the larger tool while a small shape requires the Shape Mate. Place the shape on the moulding pad. With the round end of the white Character Shaper held at a slight angle to the moulding pad ....
move in a circle around the outside edge of the shape coming into the centre like a spiral.

Firm, not hard, downwards pressure is required. It is the speed in the centre that assists with the **"cup character"**. Some larger shapes use both the Character Shaper and then the Shape Mate when severe **"cup character"** is required.
I cannot emphasize too much, the importance of the spiral action. Around the outer edge twice then like a spiral into the centre, picking up speed as you reach the centre.

Beehive Character: As above, turn the shape over when completed.

Curling Character: Place the punched shape on the edge of the moulding pad. Hold the needle end of DEET, flat/horizontal on the petal. With downwards pressure, move it firmly across the edge of the shape on the pad. A slight backwards and forwards movement may assist. The edge will curl giving you an **"inwards curling"** effect. The shape will flip over most times. Turn the shape over and repeat the above on another edge for **"outwards curling".** One edge inwards with the other edge outwards gives a realistic effect. Curl the top of the side edges only, not straight up the sides. Use flat, the length of the needle, not the point.
NOTE: Flat/horizontal means flat like the workbench/table. Held at an angle will not create "curling".

Curving Character:

A petal/leaf can be turned over to give character on the reverse side. The tip from the front and the stem section from the back allows the shape to move in different directions.
Use the half moon technique above. The tool is stroked along the length of the petal/leaf, not the width.

Collar:

The average collar is made from a strip of matching paper, 2mm. wide by 8cm. long. Wind the paper on top of itself around the handle of a paintbrush and glue the end. Slide the collar off the handle and glue the pointed base of the flower inside the circle. The collar diameter should be approximately 5mm. This allows the flower to stand upright. A collar is also used to give height to a flower. Individual collar heights are made to suit the arrangement.

Wedge:

Make a collar and when completed, pinch one end of the shape so as to form a wedge. Push the opposite end inwards if a higher wedge is needed, or squeeze to flatten. The length of the paper will vary according to the size of the wedge.

Combine flat and angled flowers to reproduce the beauty of nature.

Character Shaping Instructions *continued:*

Wrap around Character:

The shaping in this character breaks the fibres in the paper making it easy to curve into another shape. The needle end of DEET is used. The tool is held in the horizontal position.

The palm of your hand above the body of the tool.

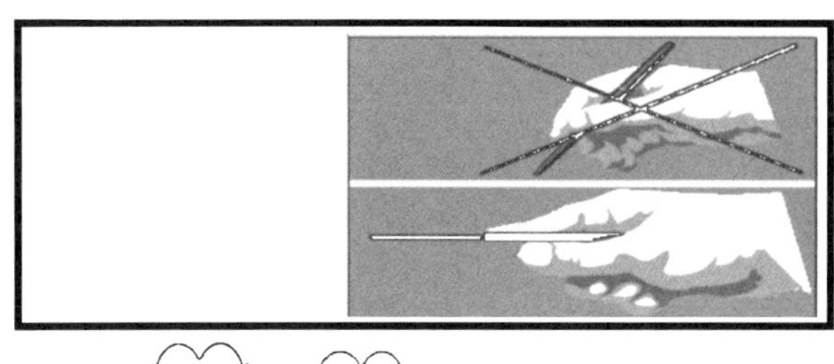

The tool pivots on the section where the needle joins the handle.

The tip of the needle sweeps around the edge of the shape like the hand of a clock turning backwards.

Place the punched shape on the moulding pad, near the edge. Place the tool in position, as shown in the first diagram.

Pivot like the hand of the clock, and finish in the position seen in the second diagram.

The third diagram shows the shape wrapped around the needle.

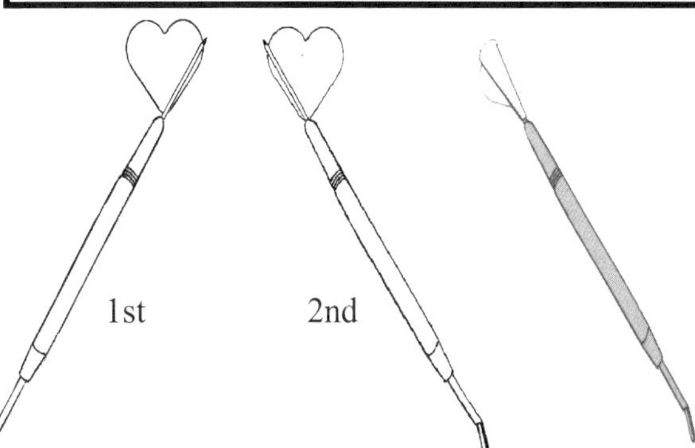

The completed shape is similar to an icecream cone.

Pendulum:

This character is the reverse of "wrap around". Deet is held flat in the horizontal position. Place the shape onto the moulding pad.

The flat needle is placed on top of the shape, so the point of the needle is touching the base of the shape. The white circle on the Balloon shape indicates the position. This would be the same for any punched shape.

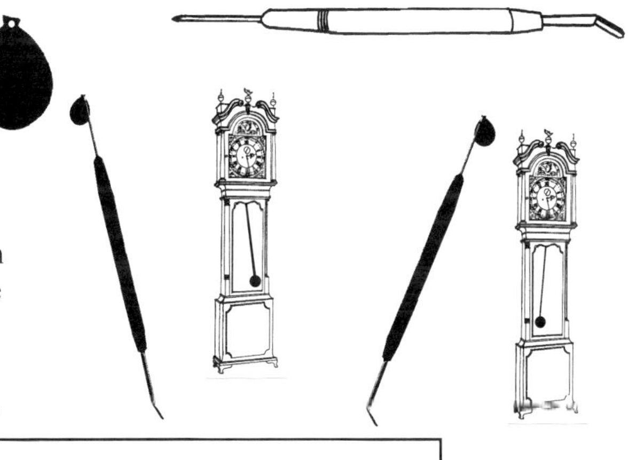

Pivot without lifting the point and sweep the length of the needle across the shape and back again like a pendulum in a Grandfather clock.
Use a little downwards pressure.
Repeat until the desired effect has been achieved.

> NOTE: The angle of the tool when beginning the shaping and again when completed. It is the same as the pendulum in the Grandfather clock.

This shaping is ideal for some small petals requiring character. The petals will not wrap around the needle.

Wave: 

Lengthwise, to the front only, the centre of the shape has "**halfmoon character**". Turn the shape over. Give "halfmoon character" to the paper on both sides of the previously moulded shape. Because the tool is near the edge of the shape, only half of the "halfmoon" shaping can be achieved. This creates "wave character".

Petal Arranging:

Petals can overlap each other. Some flowers have petals behind each other. The explanation below is to give you an idea of how to find the correct position. Follow the instructions for each project as to the petals' pattern. Arrange the position of petals by thinking of them as the hands on a clock. Glue each petal to the base as follows:

- **4 petals** - One on the 3, 6, 9 and 12.
- **5 petals -** A petal every 12 minutes.
- **6 petals** -Petal on the 2, 4, 6, 8, 10, 12.
- **7 petals** - Place approximately 9 minutes apart.
- **8 petals -** As for 4 petals. Adhere an extra shape between each of the four petals.

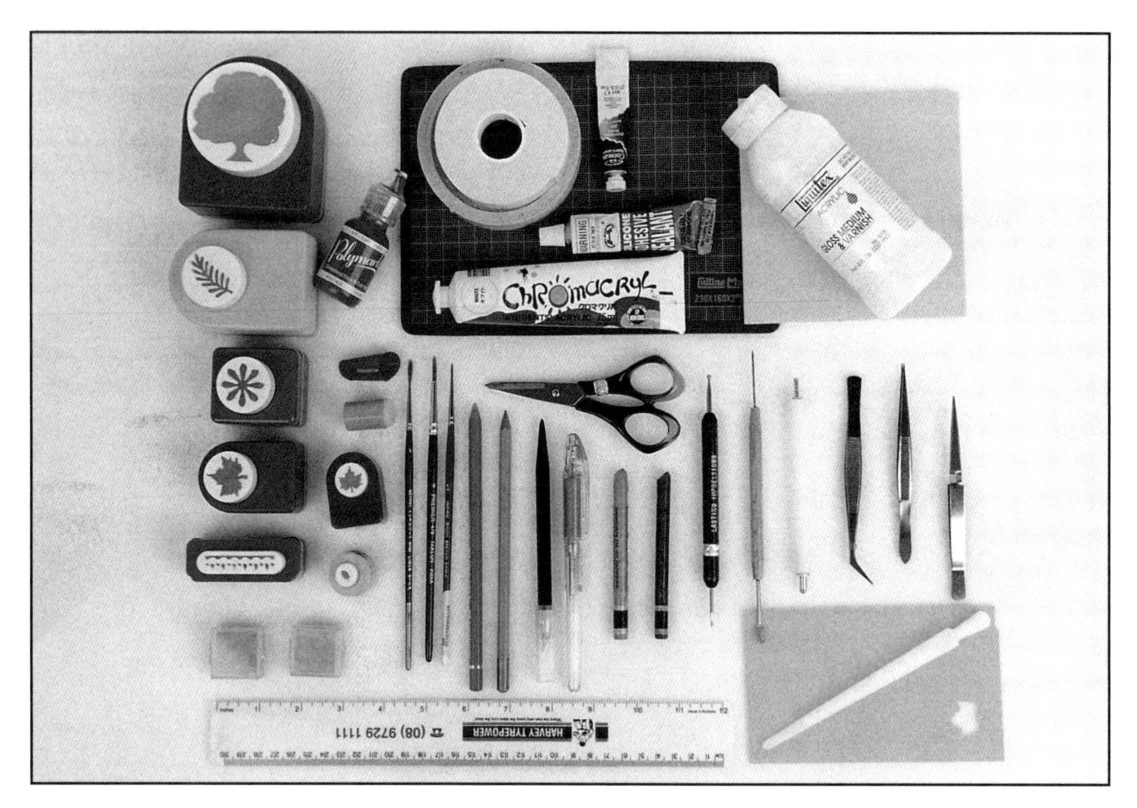

Punch Chart.

Check your punch against the chart below for size verification. When the button on the top of the punch fits into the shape, I will call the punch by that size.

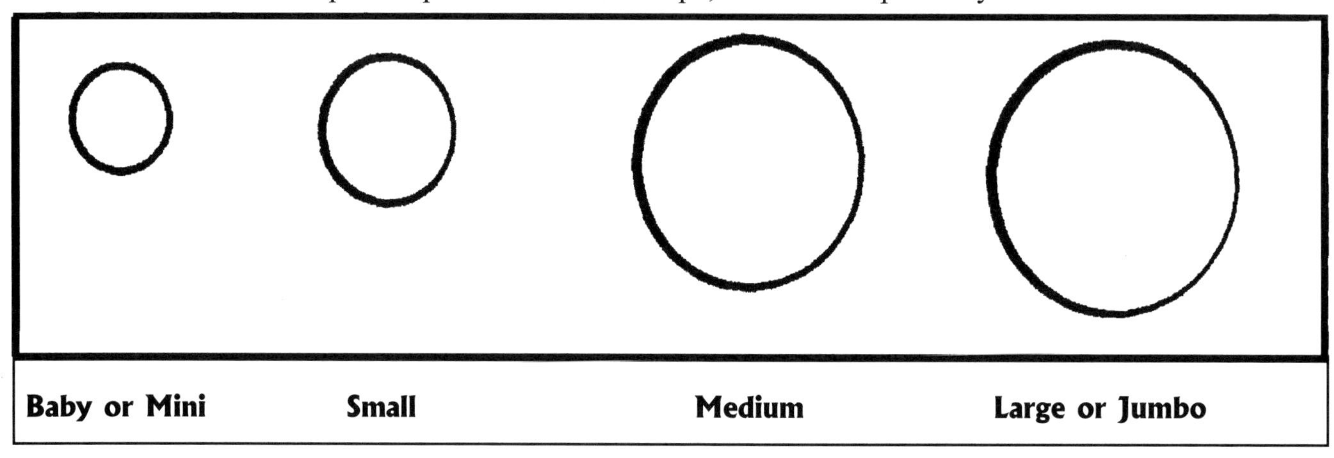

Information.

Abbreviation: Deet is **D**ouble **E**nded **E**tching **T**ool.

Paper: The paper does not have to be a certain weight. The colour is more important. Computer weight paper is recommended. Acid free paper is not required.

Scrapbooking: Acid free paper **is** required in Scrapbooking when the paper is touching the photograph.

PVA: This is a white, wood glue.

Stems: Glue two strips of paper together to give strength.

Punches: Some punched shapes are similar to each other in outline. If you have a shape similar to one utilized in my book, substitute it. If the result is pleasing continue to use it.

Support: Sit in a supportive chair and take regular breaks for exercise.

Light: Work in good day light. At night, an overhead light throws shadows. Combine it with a lamp. The light should shine below your eye level onto your hands and work area.

Equipment.

1. Craft Punches:

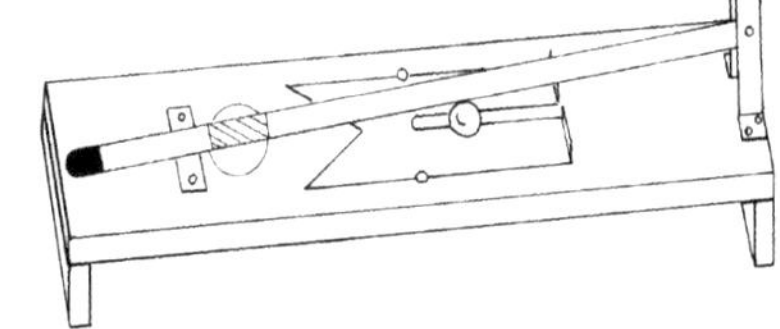

These can be purchased from Craft Shops. The range of designs is large and varied. Start with two or three and slowly build up a collection. The use for these punches is only limited by your imagination.
New punches are continually coming onto the market, check your store at regular intervals for new arrivals.
Various brands are available, if the shape is similar to the instructions it can be used.
A small collection will create many types of Flowers, Birthday/Christmas Cards and more. As you read through this book the better you will understand how to use them to their full advantage.
The Leone Em Punch Master, shown in the diagram above, is designed to make punching shapes simple for those with arthritic hands or similar.

2. Moulding Pads:
A computer Mouse pad can be used, but for better results buy a moulding pad similar to a Paper Tole pad.
My pad is 13.5cm square and yellow in colour. The texture is important not the size/colour.

3. Character Shaper:
The white coloured tool is called Character Shaper. Both ends of this tool are used. It has a large rounded end for moulding "cup character". The other end is a small curved half circle for shaping petals, bells and more. There is a thumb grip in the handle of the rounded end of the tool, this allows you to place more pressure on the tool when required and stops your hand from sliding down.

4. Shape Mate:

The Leone Em Shape Mate, shown in illustration, is a large, double ended embossing tool. The Shape Mate or a leather embossing tool, is utilized for moulding the medium flowers, e.g. Hydrangea. Double ended tools are good value as both ends are different in size. The smooth, rounded end of a large paintbrush can be used as a substitute.

5. Embossing Tools:
Size: Top - small: This tool is used for embossing when parchment/vellum is involved in the design.
Bottom: This tool shapes the very small punched pieces such as those from the Baby Flower Punch.

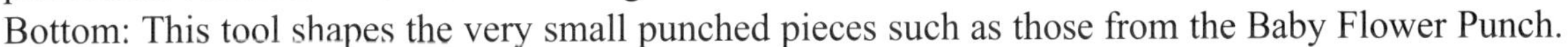

6. DEET:
A double ended tool for pottery is of great value. The pointed end is strong and more pressure can be applied when required. It is used flat for veining leaves and curling petals.
Regard the spade end as a long finger nail that can reach and hold flowers/leaves in difficult to get at places. A darning needle is a good substitute but is not as easy to handle.

7. Small Scissors:
Scissors with pointed blade tips are the best. Check the scissors before purchasing.
They should open and close with ease. I do not recommend embroidery scissors with rounded blade tips.

8. Water Soluble Colours:
Water soluble pencils, crayons or Artist's paints and markers. Check for acid free when scrapbooking.
The use of water soluble colours will create life-like appearance.

9. Paints:
Paints in small plastic bottles with a nozzle are ideal. You can also use a brush with any type of paint. The paint is used for stamens or the tips of stamens and gives a realistic effect.
White and yellow paint plus Cotman Dioxazine Violet Water Colour are required for creating Violets.

10. Paint brushes: Sizes, 0, 2, 4. Expensive artist brushes are not required while cheap brushes are not good value. Medium priced brushes will earn their keep and accomplish the desired effects. Size 0 is for fine work. Size 2 is used most. Size 4 is for dampening the paper or giving an all over tint to the shapes.
A fine liner brush is invaluable.

Equipment continued:

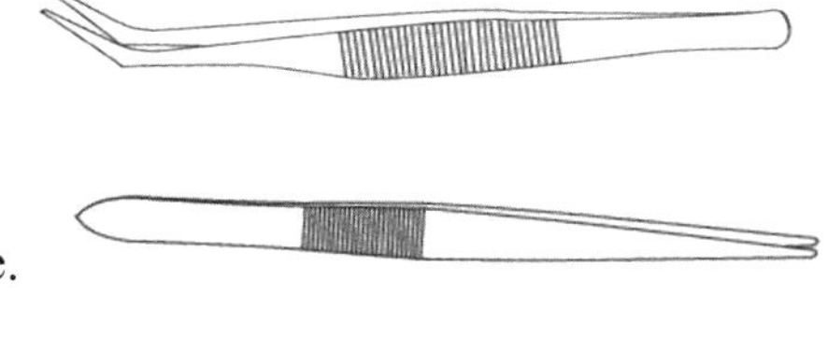

11. Tweezers:

(a) Tweezers with pointed, angled tips are your third hand. Test before buying. Hold, between your thumb and middle finger, the outside of the tweezers' half way along the arms. The centre should close with no gap between the blades when a little pressure is applied. With use, the tweezers become more pliable.

(b) Straight tweezers with pointed tips are also recommended. Chemist shop tweezers are not recommended for this craft.

(c) The closed tweezers are invaluable. When you release your grip the tweezers close. Very useful when rolling or turning the shape, as the tweezers hold the shape without finger pressure. In addition, the tweezers hold glued portions together to dry, allowing you to work on another segment of the flower at the same time. Use these tweezers to hold your card in a closed position when working.

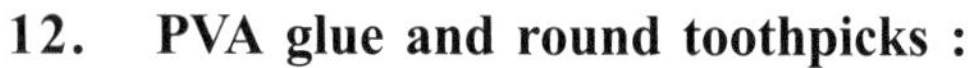

12. PVA glue and round toothpicks :
Pour the PVA glue into a small film container and dip the end of the toothpick into the glue when gluing. Place the toothpick into a small jar when not in use. This will keep the end of the toothpick clean. When your work is completed for the day, place the lid on the film container.

13. Coloured paper for the flowers leaves and cardboard for making the cards:
Various shades including flock paper.

14. Fancy Scissors: Can be used for borders but not 100% necessary.

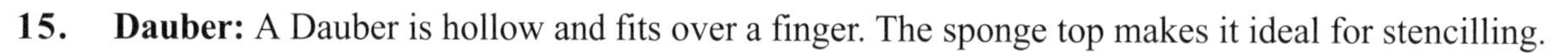

15. Dauber: A Dauber is hollow and fits over a finger. The sponge top makes it ideal for stencilling.

16. Sea Sponge:
A sea sponge is an asset because it is easy to use when combined with the water soluble pencils/ crayons. Add water to the palette, dab the Sea Sponge into the colour and pat onto the card for a stippled background or onto the petals/leaves to create a variegated appearance.

17. Craft Knife and Self Healing Mat: For cutting the cards or base patterns.

18. Light Box: (or substitute). Use this item when paper embossing (dry embossing).

19. Heat embossing: Embossing powder and heat source plus felt tipped markers for colouring.

20. Silicone glue: For cake decorating project.

21. Craft aluminium and copper: Illustrations in colour on pages 18 and 31.

22. Parchment/Vellum: Illustration and instructions on pages 28 and 29.

Sundries:
Ruler, set square, masking tape, pencil, sharpener and rubber. Double sided sticky tape and double sided sticky mounting tape. Gloss Craft Paint. Piece of felt approximately 5mm thick or similar. Gold metallic felt tipped pens.

Flowers

Always create a number of the same flower. The flowers in excess of your requirement are placed in a container for use in the future. The reason is simple. The more you construct the faster you become. Make 1 flower which you could consider difficult and you will avoid it. Make between 5 to 6 and you will become so at ease with the flower because you understand it's character, you will look for it when creating other cards. From time to time I have it said to me "I'll never make this flower again". A short time later with 4 or 5 flowers completed everyone is relaxed and words like "This is easy" brings smiling faces to the fore.

Lilium regale *(front cover)*

Punches required: Super Giant Lilium Feathers Large/Jumbo Hoki's Fern

Mini/Baby Flower

Super Giant Peublo Vase

Paper: White paper for the Liliums, green for the fern leaves and Deep Purple for the tiny flowers.
Paints: Water soluble pencils/crayons (a) yellow (b) purple with a touch of red, chart shown inside the back cover.
Shapes per flower: One Lilium Feathers per large flower. Nine flowers required.
Thirty six Mini Flowers for the tiny flowers on stems.
Leaves: Twenty three, green Hoki's Fern for the arrangement.
Mat board: This design is ready to frame. The mat board is 20.8 cm/8 ¼"wide and 27.2 cm/10 ¾" high.
Oblong cut out - 11cm/4 ¼" wide and 16.5 cm/6½" high. Measurements have been rounded off.

Vase:

1. Punch three vases from light purple cardboard. These join together to make one large vase.
2. Adhere two vases together as seen in diagram 2.
3. Adhere the third on top of Step 2. The base line appears as one shape, diagram 3.

Diagram 1

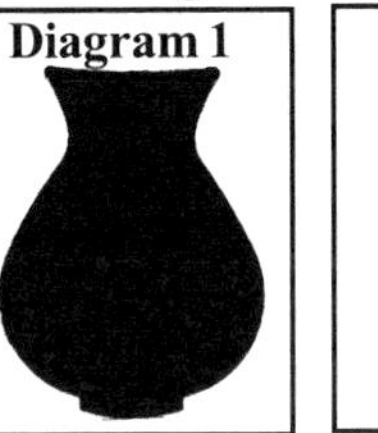

Diagram 2

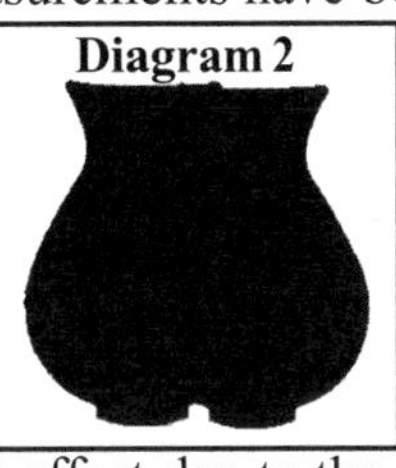

Diagram 3

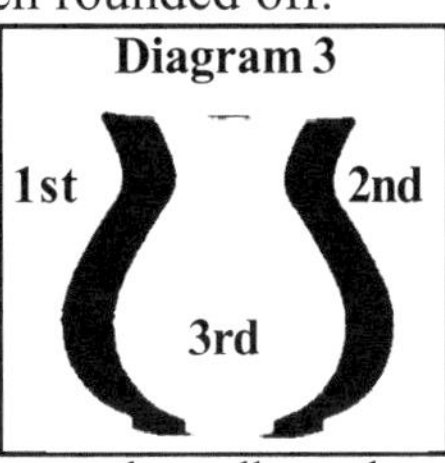

4. On the pad, give **"slight half moon character"**. This requires a little effort due to the layered cardboard.
5. To the centre of the combined vases, at the back, adhere double sided mounting tape lengthwise. Several layers are necessary to lift the vase 1cm/3/8th" off the mat board. Measure height at the centre base line.
6. Remove the backing and join onto the matboard as seen in the coloured illustration on the front of the book.

Optional: Attach a fine lined paper to the mat board behind the flowers as seen in the illustration on the front cover.

Lilium *regale*:

1. Punch nine, white Lilium Feathers shapes. Use water soluble pencils/crayons to colour (a) part of one side in yellow, (b) the other, in purple with a touch of red, pale then deeper with the second coat. See the inside of the back cover for the Colour Chart. Allow to dry.
2. Place unto the moulding pad and give **"wave character"** to the length of each petal.
3. Use the straight tweezers and curve the shape, from the top, into a cone shape.
4. Adhere the top flap to secure the shape leaving no gap, diagram 4.

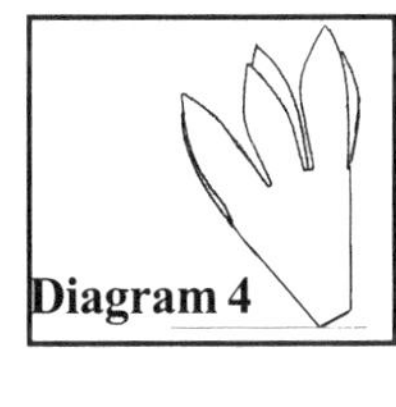

Diagram 4

Note: The yellow colouring is the inside of the flower.

5. Add a green stem to the base of each flower. The stem is two layers of paper glued together.

Stamens:

6. This variety of Lilium has seven stamens. Trim a piece of green paper to the exact size shown in diagram 5. The first stamen is the longest. The other six vary in shorter lengths.
7. **"Roll"** into a tight coil, the base of the stamens with the closed tweezers. The left end is the glue flap.
8. Tip the longest stamen with green paint to form a round shape, diagram 6.
9. The other six stamens are tipped with orange paint. The colouring is longer in length and not round.

Diagram 5

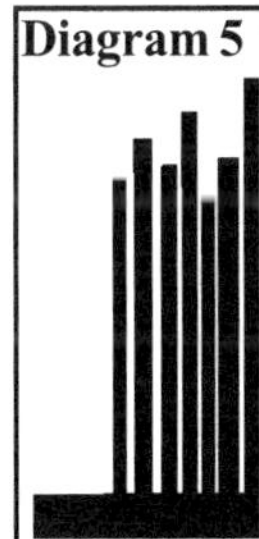

Diagram 6

Note: Tip the stamens in the following manner.

a. Splay the stamens into a fan shape.
b. Pour a little paint onto the top of a small lid.
c. Holding the stamens with the closed tweezers, turn them upside down and dip the tips into the pain
d. Allow to dry and repaint in the same manner to build the tip into the correct shape.

10. Allow to dry.

Tiny Flowers:

11. Place the Mini Flower shapes on the moulding pad and give **"cup character"**.
12. Cut nine green stems. Double the paper and glue together for added strength.
13. Adhere three to five shapes per stem, diagram 7. Allow to dry.

Diagram 7

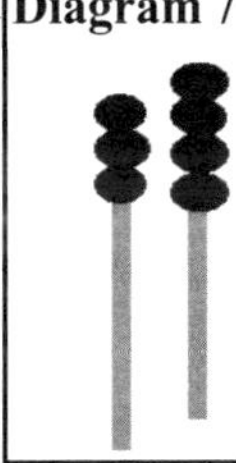

Assembling the design:

14. Adhere the Liliums near the top of the vase as a starting point. Use collars and wedges where necessary.
15. Work, from the edge of the vase to the top of the design, until the Liliums are adhered into position.
16. Give the stems of the tiny flowers **"gently curving character"**.
17. Add the tiny flowers and the Fern leaves.

Versatility.

Ideas using Floral Punch Craft and/or Punches.

It is amazing where Floral Punch Craft ventures, over the rainbow and beyond. This page is an Ideas page to spark the imagination, with the versatility of this craft, whether a beginner or a seasoned handcrafter.

Jewellery

Punches required:

Small Heart   Small Birch   Super Giant Oval

The tiny Brooch resembles porcelain.
After painting, several times, with a water based, clear, acrylic finish gloss the paper becomes hardened giving a porcelain appearance.
Nine small Roses and one bud are required. Each Rose is created with ten Small Hearts. The bud requires three Small Hearts plus twelve small green, Small Birch Leaves.
The base for the broach is several shapes punched with the Super Giant Oval.
The ovals are adhered together for strength.
A brooch clip is firmly attached at the back of the combined oval shapes.
The layout is simple and the instructions for the small Rose is the same as the larger Rose, Flower No.15 in Floral Punch Craft, the first Leone Em book. Matching ear rings can also be created.

Badge

Simple, flat Floral Punch Craft design. Could be a name badge or just for fun.

Stamp

1. Punch your favourite shapes from thin fun foam.
2. Glue the shape to the bottom of a block of wood and use the same as a conventional stamp.
   A lid from a container, providing the lid is perfectly flat, can be substituted for the block of wood.

Face Painting

1. Use a piece of Mylar or similar to suit the punch being used. If Mylar or similar is unavailable, use cardboard. Never force a punch to cut unsuitable materials.
2. Use a sea sponge/dauber and face paint to colour the template's shape.

Suggestions:
Use for children's birthday parties, fund raising and more. Father Christmas, Christmas Tree and Holly make a wonderful combination at Christmas time. Lightweight Mylar or substitute is required when punching the Reindeer due to the antlers. For children who do not like face painting, a Christmas scene on their arm is the answer.

Sand Painting

The scene, on the front of the Greeting Card, in the illustration is achieved with coloured sand and Jac Paper. The Sand is available in a multitude of colours.
Jac paper is similar to double sided sticky tape and comes in A4 size sheets.
To Sand Paint: peel the protective sheet off the Jac Paper and sprinkle the sand as if sprinkling salt on chips. Rub, in a circular motion, with your finger. Shake off the excess.
For the greeting card in the illustration, various punches come into play.
Trees, medium and large, Daisiy, both sizes, Large House and Large Oak Leaf.
The hills also, are sand coated Jac paper. They a cut free hand.
The shapes are punched from the Jac Paper and sand painted.
Flowers:
Punch the Daisies from single sided Jac paper, sprinkle with the sand. Remove the sand from the centre and mould into "cup character" to the centre only.
Centre: Punch from yellow paper, no sand is required, one shape per flower.
The Mini Flower shape has beehive character. Adhere to the centre of each flower.

Pin Pricking

The coloured illustration, using parchment, is on page 31.
The punched shapes are placed on the back of the front cover.
Create the design by placing the shapes in a pleasing layout.
Hold securely with masking tape.
Pin prick around the edge of each punched shape.
Remove the tape and the punched shapes.
Add colour with the water soluable crayons/pencils. To blend the colours, use a cotton wool bud dampened slightly and dried off with a facial tissue.
Cut the edge with fancy scissors and emboss.
Complete with a coloured insert.

Parchment

Use the same instructions as for paper. The parchment/vellum is different and requires coaxing at times but the end result is worth the extra attention. See the above instructions when colouring. The coloured illustration is on page 31.

Decoration

The decoration in the illustration brings together Floral Punch Craft, driftwood, carved wooden dish and pottery birds.

As a table piece or on a window sill, the arrangement brings colour and enchantment into any room. Makes a wonderful gift.

Fairies.

Punches required: Small Egg and Shell Medium Heart Frame Butterfly

Shapes and colours per Fairy:
One, magenta Frame Butterfly and Shell.
Two, brown Eggs.
Four, pale pink Hearts.

Diagram 1.
4th 3rd 2nd 1st

Dress:

1. Trim the four Hearts as shown in diagram 1. The hem is cut with Deckle scissors.
2. Colour the edge of the hem with a dark pink, felt tipped marker.

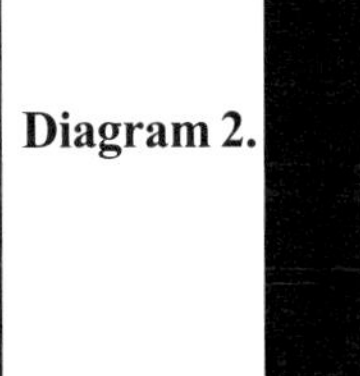

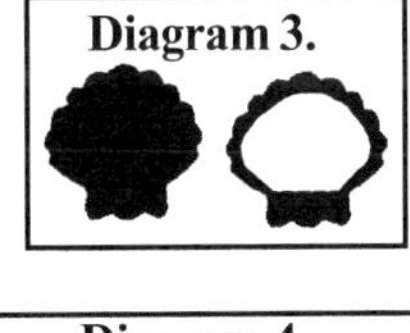

Base shape:

1. Cut a piece of white cardboard to the exact shape shown in diagram 2.

Wings:

1. Remove the Butterfly from the frame.
2. Trim, to a smooth edge, the body and lower wings.

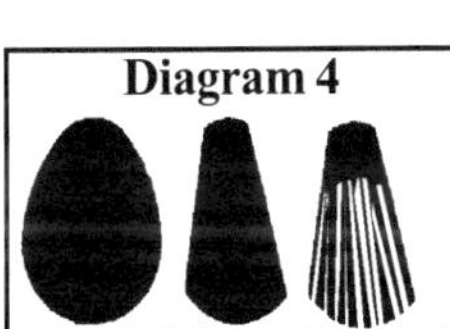

Head:

1. Remove a portion of the Shell shape, shown in diagram 3.
2. Trim and fringe one brown Egg shape, shown in diagram 4.
3. Adhere the base of Step 1 to the top of Step 2, diagram 5.
4. Glue Step 3 on top of the second brown Egg to allow the brown hair to show under the head piece.
5. If required, remove any excess from the sides of the second Egg shape.

Combine:

1. Glue the top of the each dress shape to the base shape, in order, commencing with the first. Each shape overlaps the other, going up the base shape like rungs in a stepladder. Allow a portion of each shape to show.
2. Adhere the wings in position.
3. Adhere the head to allow the hair to fall over the centre of the wings. Trim the brown Egg shape, under the head piece, should any protrude on either sides of the head piece.

Cake Decorating.

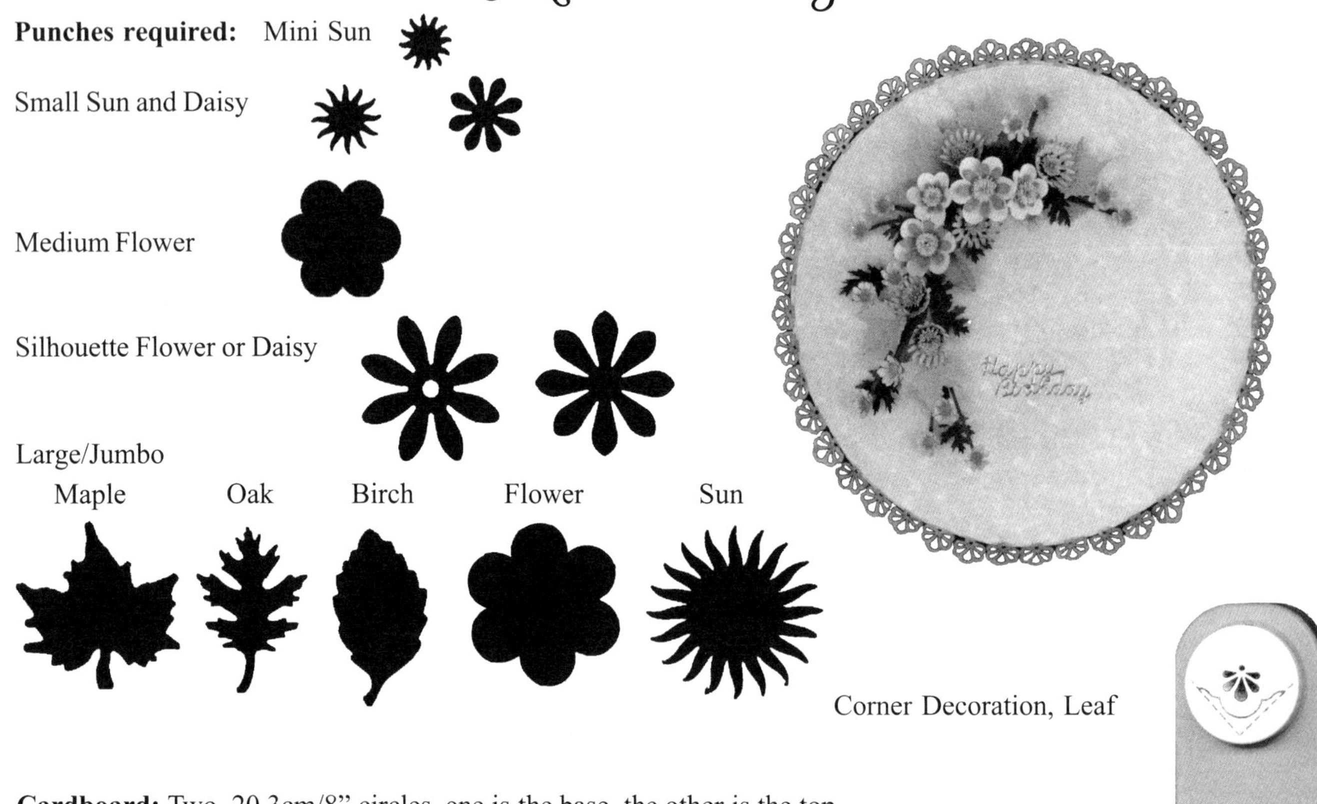

Cardboard: Two, 20.3cm/8” circles, one is the base, the other is the top.
Note: Laminate the two circles if re-use is an option.
Paper: Apricot toning for the entire top, including the lace work. Black for the inside section of the Sun flower. Three greens for the leaves and stems.

Number of flowers:
Illustration 1, two flowers.
Illustration 2, two flowers.
Illustration 3, fourteen flowers,
Illustration 4, five flowers.

Flowers:
Note: The first two flowers, Illustrations No. 1 and No. 2, are different in size only.

1. Punch two each of the Large/Jumbo Flowers and Daisy or Silhouette Flowers.
2. Place the Daisy shapes on the moulding pad and give **“cup character”**.
3. Cut the Flower shape as shown in diagram 1.
4. Place the shapes on the moulding pad and give **“halfmoon character”** to each petal.
5. Adhere Step 2 inside Step 4.
6. Repeat the Steps above using the Medium Flower and the Small Daisy.
7. Punch five Large/Jumbo Suns.
8. Colour in deep orange,the tip of each ray with the Leone Em stamp or colour by hand.
9. With the scissors, make a cut between two rays into the centre, diagram 2.
10. Give “**severe cup character**” to the five Sun shapes on the moulding pad.
(a) The cut will allow one cut edge to go behind the other.
(b) Glue the base of three rays at the back. This secures the shape into a tighter cup shape. There are seventeen rays plus the three back rays.
11. Punch five black, Small Sun shapes.
12. Mould “cup character” and adhere inside Step 10(b).
13. Punch two Small Daisies per flower. Fourteen flowers required.
14. Place the shapes on the moulding pad.
(a) Fourteen shapes require “**cup character**;.
(b) The remainder require “**severe cup character**”.
15. Punch one Mini/Baby Sun per flower and give “**severe cup character**”.
16. Adhere Step 14(b) inside Step 14(a).
17. Adhere Step 15 inside Step 16. This completes the small flower.

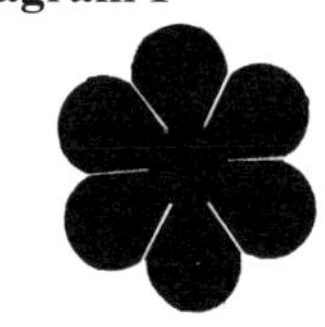

Flower Identification:

Identify the large flower by the white circle.
The flower and the identifying circle is seen in the illustration opposite.

Illustration No.1

Identifying the flowers and their placement, assists when assembling the layout.

Commence with the two, larger flowers and work out from this point.

Identify the smaller flower by a white circle with a black circle in the centre.

Illustration No. 2

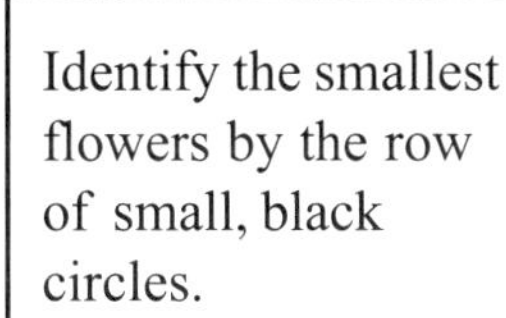

Identify the smallest flowers by the row of small, black circles.

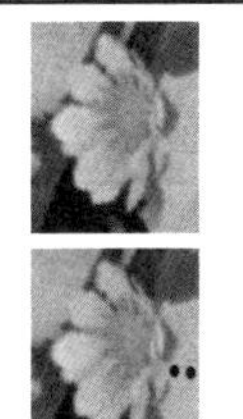

Illustration No. 3

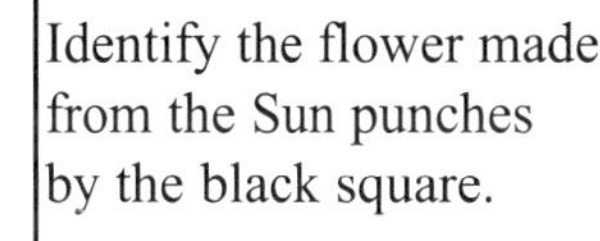

Identify the flower made from the Sun punches by the black square.

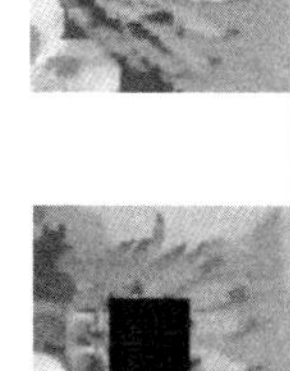

Illustration No. 4

Fringing the centres:
Apricot shades

1. Cut a 4.5mm/ 3/16" strip of paper by the length of an A4 sheet and fringe finely. Cut the length in half.
2. **"Roll"** each of the fringed strips into a tight coil. Fluff the fringing outwards with the thumbs.
3. Glue inside the large flowers, one per flower. Illustration 1 above.
4. Repeat the three steps above for the smaller flower in Illustration 2.
   Note: Trim the length to10cm/4" before **"rolling"**.
5. Flower No. 3, fringing is not necessary.
6. Repeat Steps 1 and 2 using a strip the same length by 6mm wide. The flower is in Illustration No 4.
   Note: Make five, fringed coils for the five flowers.
7. Glue inside the large Sun flowers, Illustration No. 4.

Lace: Corner Decorating Punch, Leaf.

Note: This punch requires a corner of the paper if the removable sides are in place.

1. Punch forty three shapes, diagram 1.
2. Trim, each shape, as follows:
   (a) Excess from sides, diagram 2. This action removes the top excess at the same time.
   (b) Trim around the entire shape, diagram 3.
4. Paint/spray, with a paper sealer, both sides of all the shapes.
   Allow to dry.
5. Bend the shank at right angles to the lace pattern.
6. Use PVA glue to adhere the shanks to bottom of the cake top, in a circle, around the edge.

For neatness: Cover the entire base with a cardboard circle. *Optional.*

Diagram 1

Diagram 3

Diagram 2

Optional: Place the cake top up-side-down on an up-side down cake tin when adhering the lace shapes.
Note: Two coats of the sealer will give the lace shapes more strength especially if the cake top is to be re-used.

Laminated Cake Tops:

(a) Adhere the shanks with double sided sticky tape to the bottom of the laminated top circle.
(b) Adhere the base and top laminated circles together with double sided sticky tape.

Lilacs.

Punch required: Super Giant Lilac and Daphne combination punch.

Paper: Two shades of Lilac are required, one pale and the other a little deeper in colour.
Card: Purple cardboard, size when folded, 16.5cm/6 1/2" high by 10.5cm/4 1/8" wide.

Shapes: Many shapes are required. From the pale lilac paper, punch out forty petals from the section of the punch seen in the diagram on the right. Punch fifteen in the deeper lilac. More can be punched when required. These shapes are the blooms.
Leaves: Punch green leaves from the section of the punch shown in diagram. If other shapes are punched at the same time, keep for use at a later date.

Cone base:

1. From a light weight cardboard, cut six, white or lilac square shapes to the size shown in diagram 1. The black circle indicates the position of the tweezers.
2. Place the closed tweezers into position as seen in diagram 2.
3. Roll the tweezers over until you have a cone shaped point at the base near the tweezers.
4. Slide the tweezers' section closest to you, across the cardboard to the other side.
5. Glue the edge and adhere, See diagram 3.
6. Trim off the excess. The shape is now a cone.

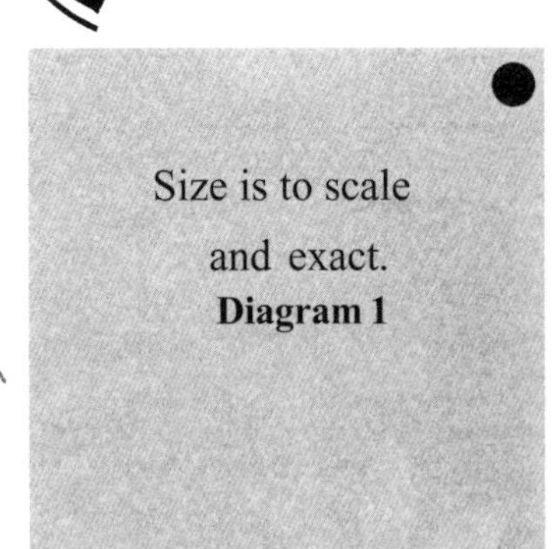

Diagram 1

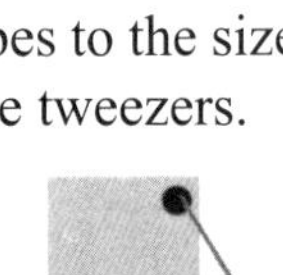
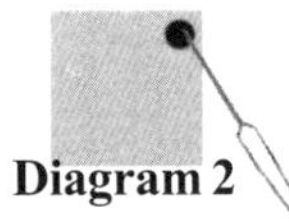
Diagram 2

Diagram 3

7. Trim 7mm/5/16"off the base of three cones.
8. These three cones have four slits cut to the size shown in diagram 4.
9. Open the slits outwards to form three flaps, diagram 5.

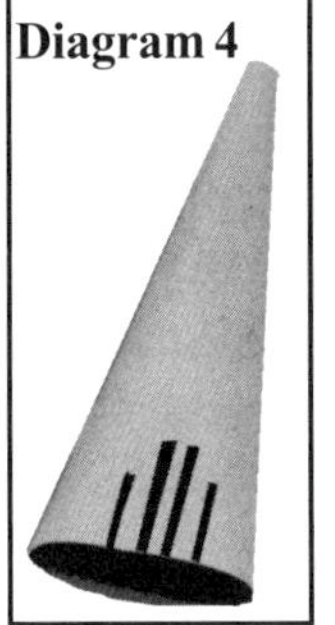
Diagram 4

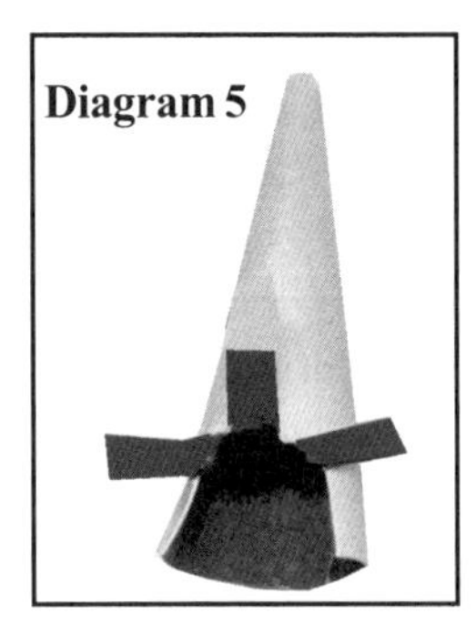
Diagram 5

10. Adhere the smaller cone to the side of the larger cone. The flaps are indicated by the paler shade. It is the flaps that are adhered to the larger cone, diagram 6.
11. The result is three, double cones. Turn over, one combined shape. The smaller section of the double cone is now on the opposite side to the other two double cones, diagram 7. These are the base shapes, onto which the Lilac flowers are glued, completed.

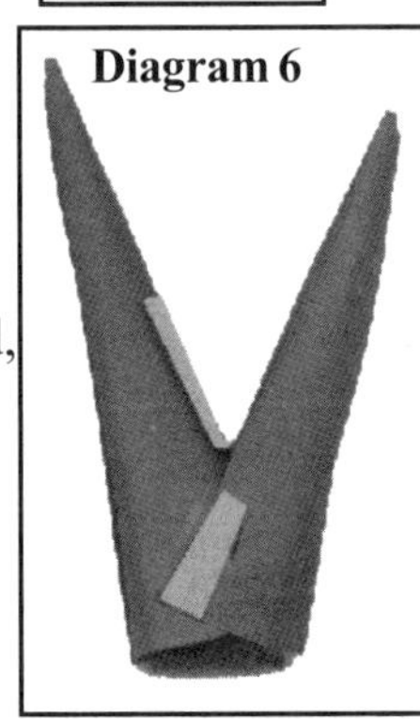
Diagram 6

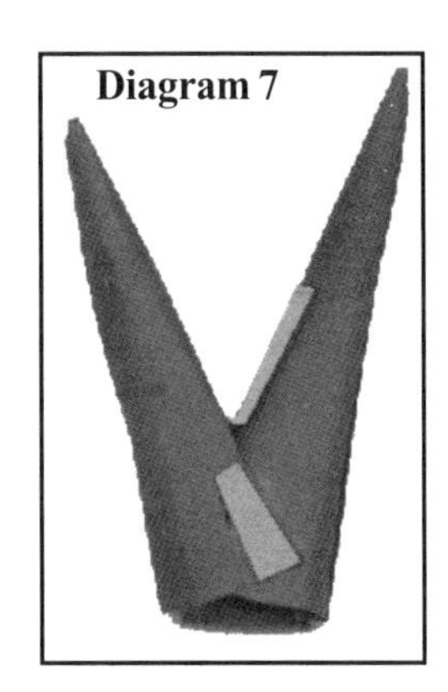
Diagram 7

Blooms:

12. Place the blooms on the pad and give "**severe cup character".**
13. Adhere to the double cone shapes with a few scattered, deeper coloured shapes. The shapes are not required on the lower, back sections of the cones. Diagram 8 shows a completed double cone.
14. Adhere one of the double cones onto the card. Follow the coloured illustration for the position. The design on top of the base card is on page 46.
15. Push the base flat with your finger. This allows the second, combined cone to be adhered at an angle, across the base. This prevents the Lilacs protruding too far.
16. Push the second base flat and adhere the third completed shape into position.

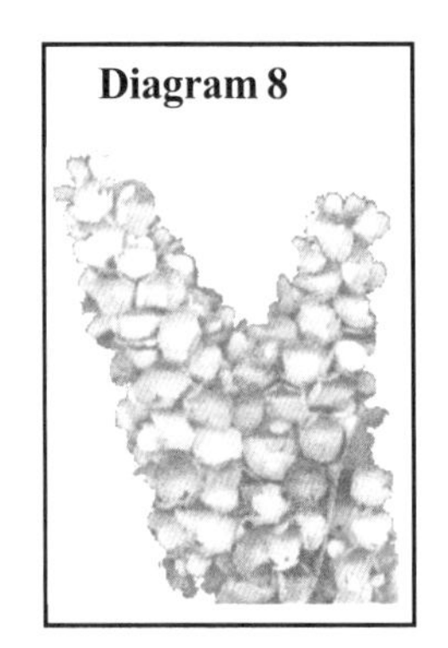
Diagram 8

Leaves: The Lilac leaves grow in pairs.

17. Punch sixteen large and four small leaves from green paper.
18. Cut a pale strip of green paper to shape seen here.
19. Adhere the shape between two small leaves. This is new growth.
20. Arrange and adhere the leaves where required.
21. Cover the base of the completed cone shapes with a stem of leaves.
22. Follow the **coloured illustration** for placement of leaves, if required.

Lilacs

A Silver Lining

A Basket of Violets

Iris

Flowering Cherry Plum, *Prunis blireiana*

Flowering Cherry Plum *Prunis blireiana.*

Designed for a special, courageous individual, Joy. I am proud to be her friend.

Punches required: Small Foot  Medium Heart 

Paper: Pale Pink for blossoms and insert. Red (with pink toning) for the stamens called Coro Crimson.

Mat: Pink mat board cut to the size, 16cm/6¼" in width by 20cm/8" in height.
Cut out oval is 12cm/4¾" long by 8.5cm/3&5/16th" wide. Read "Strength" on page 22.

Cardboard: Dusty Pink for the oval's backing and the card. Attach the backing and the combined card and insert to the back of the mat board. The card creates a leg, when opened.

Diagram 1

Shapes required per bloom:

Small Foot, twelve and Medium Heart, fourteen shapes. Create five flowers and one bud.

Stamens:

1. Cut a length of pale pink paper to the exact size shown in diagram 1.
2. In red/pink water soluble pencil/crayon, paint from the base line, up to the dotted line shown in diagram 1. Allow to dry.
3. Fringe finely down to the black bar at the base. This requires fringing through part of the red/pink section, shown in diagram 2.
4. To a Coro Crimson strip, 6mm wide, glue the stamens, exact length shown in diagram 3. Note: 3mm of the stamens' base is adhered to the Coro Crimson strip. 6mm is 1/4" while 3mm is 1/8".

Diagram 2

Diagram 3
Stamens

5. Roll with the closed tweezers from the right hand end. Adhere the end to secure.
6. Gently, remove the tweezers and place one prong inside the coil, the other on the outside.
7. Open the stamens outwards with Deet and colour the tips in deep red paint. Note: Fan the stamens and dip the tips, one at a time, into the paint. Place the tweezers in a small bottle/jar until the tips are dry.

8. Roll a strip of paper, same length, width and colour as in Step 4, diagram 3 above, around Step 6.

Petals:

9. Punch twelve shapes from the Small Foot punch and trim as shown in diagram 4.

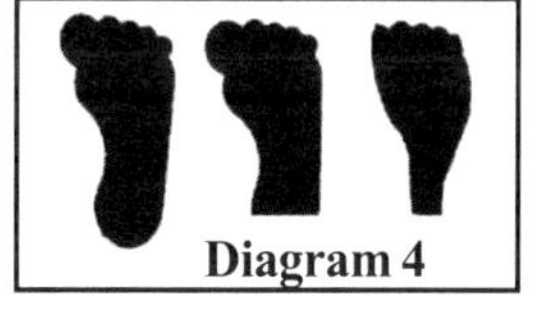
Diagram 4

10. With the Medium Heart, punch fourteen shapes. Trim as shown in diagram 5.

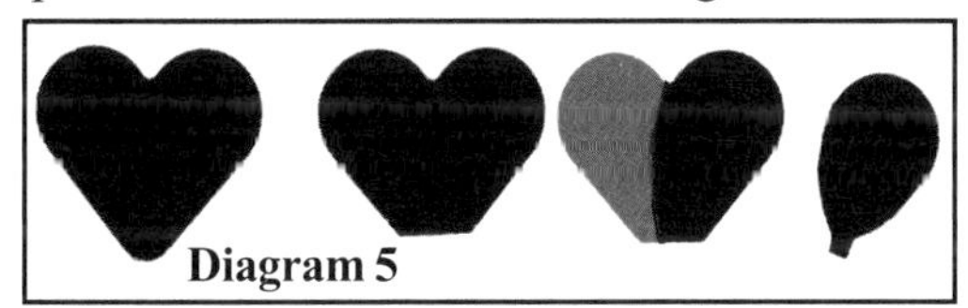
Diagram 5

11. Place the petals on the moulding pad.
12. The small petals have **"mild halfmoon character"**. Instructions on page 6.
13. Adhere the shank of each petal onto a strip of pale pink paper, 6 mm/¼" in width. The length and spacings are exact in diagram 6.

Diagram 6 | Glue | 6 petals | Nothing | 6 petals | Glue |

14. The larger petals have **"wave character"**. Instructions on page 7.

6 petals
| Glue | Nothing | | **Diagram 7**

15. Glue the shank of six petals onto a strip of pale pink paper, 6 mm/¼" in width. The black area denoted the position where the six petals are adhered. The length and spacing is exact as shown in diagram 7.

16. Glue the shanks of seven petals, onto a strip of pale pink paper, 6mm/¼" in width. The black area denoted the position where the seven petals are adhered. The length and spacing is exact as shown in diagram 8.

7 petals
Glue | Nothing | | **Glue**
Diagram 8

Flowering Cherry Plum *Prunis blireiana, continued.*

Combining the petals:

17. Place a little glue on the right hand end of the strip holding the small petals, Step 13. Adhere to Step 8. Roll around the coil held by the tweezers, Step 8. Adhere the end to secure.
18. Repeat the above Step with the petals from Step 15.
19. Repeat with the petals from Step 16, placing the first petal to cover the space where two of the previous petals touch/overlap. This avoids a gap appearing after opening the petals outwards.
20. The spare, large petal is the emergency. Use it to cover a gap, if required.
21. Gently, open the petals outwards. Arrange some the stamens to curve slightly with the tweezers.

Bud: Cut the stamens' width in half and trim the height. Roll nine small petals, on a base strip, into a bud shape.

Leaves: Leaves are not required for Cherry Plum blossoms.

Card: The card is the same size as the mat board when folded in half.

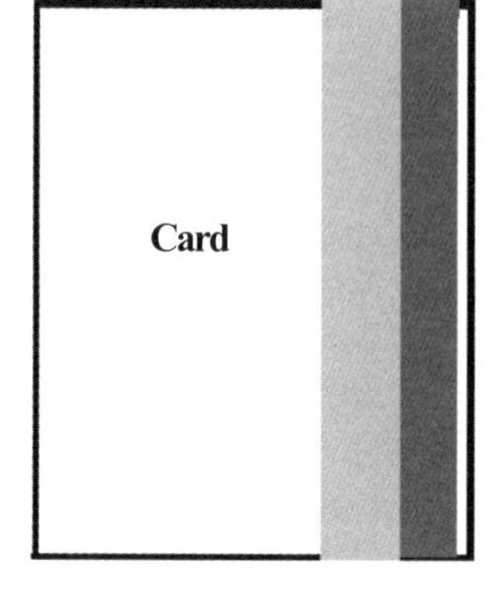

Strength:

This Step is to give strength to the card's opening edge that acts as a leg.
The opening side of the card has two layers of the **same** coloured cardboard, adhered. Use double sided sticky tape.
In the diagram the black and grey colours indicate the extra layers of cardboard.
The black layer is the width of the black and grey combined.
The grey layer is adhered on top of the black.

Combine:

Combine the mat board and card together with double side sticky tape.
Remember: Check the card is opening in the correct direction before adhering.

Twig: Choose a suitable twig from your garden. Adhere it in place with PVA glue or similar.

Assembling: Glue the flowers, in suitable positions, to the twig.

Sand the back of the twig to allow it to sit flat on the card to avoid the card twisting at a later date.

Leone Em Stamp Sets for Floral Punch Craft.

Note: STAMPS are not to scale.

Use the Leone Em stamps for instant colouring of punched shapes plus backgrounds.
Stamps come as a set of 2 Smart Blocks plus instructions.

Combine the stamps with pigment or dye ink pads.

Colour the stamp, turn up side down and place the punched shape on top of the image. Press down firmly with any flat object and remove the shape.

The large Circle stamp colours the tips of the Sun shapes while the small circle colours the body.

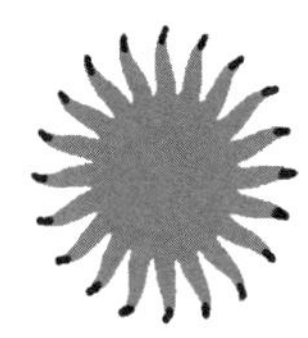

Positive stamps are for veining while the negative stamps colour the entire shape but leave the veins showing.

Large/Jumbo Horseshoe Punch Patterns

The Horseshoe Choir.

Folded card measures 17.5cm /6 3/4” by 10.5cm/ 4 1/8”.

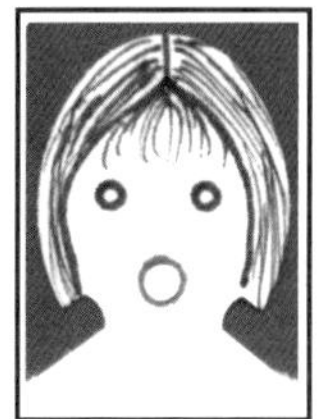

Use the above illustration as the template for completing the faces. The eyes and mouth are the exact size of the tiny Circle punches. Punch the template’s eyes and mouth. Place on top of each head and with fine felt tipped pens draw the shapes through the holes.

Above: 4 Horseshoes

Below: 6 Horseshoes

Right: Border ..... The far right edge is a strip of matching paper.

Below: 11 Horseshoe shapes are required for the circle suitable for a photograph plus circle shape for photo.

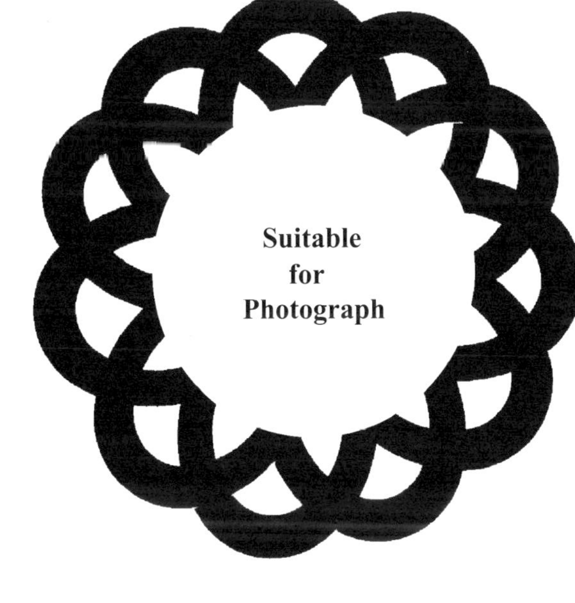

Below: 4 Horseshoes

Below: 2 Horseshoes

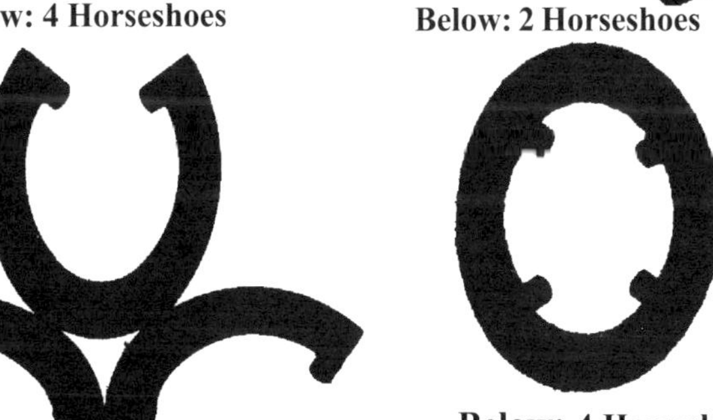

Below: 4 Horseshoes

Below: Border, 4 Horseshoes cut in half.

A Silver Lining.

Punches required:

Baby/Mini, Small Flower and Medium Flower   Small and Medium Oak Leaf

Cardboard: Folded card measures 18.5cm / 7 1/4" high by 10.5 cm / 4 1/8"wide.

Paper: Black Flock paper for the background behind the design.
Size - 17cm / 6 3/4" high by 9cm / 3 1/2" wide.
Trim the corners as shown in coloured illustration on page 18.
Insert is Outback, *Aryes Rock.*

Aluminium: Craft aluminium. This is very soft and embosses easily.
It is not aluminium foil.

Shapes: Four Baby/Mini Flowers.
Five Small Flowers.
Three Medium Flowers.
Seven Small Oak Leaves.
Eight Medium Oak Leaves.

Glue: Silicone.

Branches: Trace the branch pattern and make a template.
Use the template to mark the design.
Cut the branches to the templates markings.

Creating the Image:

1. Adhere the black flock to the front of the card with double sided sticky tape.
2. Place the Mini, Small and Medium Flower shapes on the pad.
3. In a circular motion, rub each petal section, six per flower, with a large embossing tool. This is embossing aluminium.
4. The lines shown in the diagram are also embossed. Use a fine embossing tool and draw the lines as if using a pencil.
5. Turn the shapes over. With a small embossing tool, emboss the centre only. This is called "**d**ebossing" because it is performed on the front going **d**ownwards.

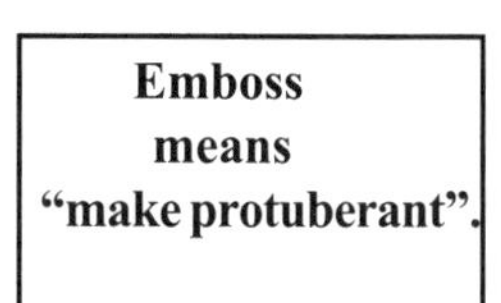

Branches and Leaves:

6. After embossing the length of the branches, adhere into position with silicone glue.
7. Place the leaves on the moulding pad.
8. With the small embossing tool, emboss the centre vein only.

Composition:

9. The Medium Flower shapes are on the lower branches.
10. All the shapes are adhered in position, with the silicone glue.
11. Follow the placement of the flowers and leaves as shown on the coloured illustration on page 18.

Instructions for Tracing Designs.

1. Any type of tracing paper is suitable. Trace on a hard surface.
2. Place the tracing paper over the design to be traced. Use masking tape to secure it to the design.
3. With a sharpened, soft black lead pencil draw the design under the tracing paper.
4. Remove the tracing paper by gently peeling off the masking tape. To avoid tearing, do not pull off sharply.
5. Turn the tracing over to the reverse side and place a scrap sheet of paper underneath. Retrace the pattern.

* *For a mirror image, retrace, as in Step 5, directly onto the card/paper where the design is required.*

6. Turn the paper over to the front. Place the tracing into the position the pattern is required and secure with masking tape.
7. Once again, retrace the design and remove the masking tape and tracing paper. The design is now on the card/paper as required.

A Basket of Violets.

Punches required: Super Giant Iris and Violet punch.
Super Giant Easter Basket, see below.

Paper: The paper for the Violets requires colouring.
Paint an A4 sheet of Juni Purple paper with Cotman Water Colour, Dioxazine Violet, water and a paintbrush. This is a pigment colour which makes it extremely difficult to colour with any other shade.
Paint both sides of the paper. See below for the leaf paper.
Allow to dry and give another coat if required.

Shapes: Fourteen flower shapes from the above coloured paper.
Punch one, green leaf for each flower.

Step by Step colouring chart is on the inside of the back cover.

Flower:

1. Paint the character lines in Dioxazine Violet on all the petals.
   Use a liner brush or Size 0. Fine lines are required.
   Use very little water for the character lines. This will make the lines stand out darker than the tinted paper.
2. Allow to dry.
3. With Size 0 paintbrush paint small white strokes onto both the side petals.
4. Repeat Step 3 on the front petal. The white extendeds a little further than the side petals.
5. When dry, repeat Steps 3 and 4 to give brilliant white strokes.
6. When dry, place all the flowers on the moulding pad.
7. With Deet, give **"pendulum character"** to the side and back petals. Vary the shapes a little by giving an extra pendulum sweep. See Pendulum character instructions on page 7.
8. Turn the shape over and give the front petal a gentle stroke along the length of the petal with the knife edge of the Character Shaper. The petal will gently curl backwards.
9. Turn the flower over again to work on the inside of the petals. With the Shape Mate, small end, give gentle **"cup character"** to the centre. Take care not to remove the previous character shaping.
10. From the same colour as the leaves, cut a stem for each flower. The paper is first doubled and glued to give extra strength to the stems.
11. Glue one flower to the end of each stem with the front petal facing down the stem.
12. Slide the tweezers along the stem and under the flower. Stop when you reach the section where the flower is glued. Turn the stem backward and at right angles to the flower.
13. Hold the stem and paint a yellow section in the centre and coming forward between the two white strokes on the front petal. Allow to dry.

Leaves:

14. Adhere a stem to each leaf. The stem is the same width as the leaf's stem and 4cm/1 & 9/16" in length.
15. Place the leaves on top of the moulding pad and give **"veining character"**.
16. With a very small embossing tool, emboss tiny veins off the side veins.

Note: Use green paper with a texture for the leaves. This creates more realistic leaves.

Card:

Prepare the card: Trace and cut the archway to fit. *Optional:* Use an AccuCut die.
Optional: Trim a strip of green hemp paper, pull the top edge to give a rough grass like appearance.
Adhere along the base line, with double sided sticky tape.

Easter Basket:

1. Punch one Easter Basket. The colour to compliment the Violets.
2. Curve the body with your fingers and attach to the card with mounting tape behind the centre section.
   Use PVA glue to adhere the top corners to the card.

Complete the card:

Adhere the Violets and leaves to the card so as to give the appearance the basket is full of Violets.
Add a complimentary coloured insert and greeting if required.

Read and practice the character shaping pages. The shaping becomes easy when you are moulding correctly.

Iris

The Iris belongs to the Iridaceae family and consist of a vast range of bulbous plants with sword like leaves. Freesia, Gladiolus and Watsonia are relatives. Irises include both desert and water plants. The Irises, while differing widely in shape and colour, do have a family similarity, which is three vertical petals, called "standards", alternating with three drooping ones, called "falls".

Punches required: Super Giant combination Iris and Violet.

Paper: White for flower and green for leaves. White computer paper is good.

Window Card: Illustrated on page19. AccuCut window die cut plus green velour for the grass, parchment (vellum) for curtains, double sided Jac paper and cream sand. The Jac paper and sand are used to give the wall a rendered appearance.

Method: Cut the Jac paper to cover the front only of the die-cut card leaving the window free. Peel the back off the Jac paper and adhere it to the card, take care not to crinkle the Jac paper. Peel the covering off the front to reveal a sticky surface. Sprinkle the sand onto the sticky surface as if you are sprinkling salt on chips. Rub, in a circular motion, with your finger. Shake off the excess. This gives a brick like finish to the house. Add a strip of green velour to the base for the grass. Emboss tiny dots on the vellum and use double sided sticky tape to adhere it to the inside of the window for the curtain. Add a wedgewood blue insert. This will add colour to the vellum.

TRY: A combination of Delft Blue Gouache and Magenta Acrylic paints on white paper for the main, Iris colour.

Cardboard: *optional,* any suitable card/cardboard.

Paint: Follow the Step by Step colouring chart on the inside back cover.
Bright yellow, a slightly deeper yellow and soft green. These colours can be painted or added with a felt tipped pen.
The main colour, Cotman Water Colour, Dioxazine Violet, must be painted. This is the same colour used for the Violets. The colour will appear different as white paper is used. Each shape is coloured separately.

Shapes: Punch three times, the section of the punch shown in the diagram. The punch contains the various shapes to create an Iris.
To imitate the coloured illustration five Iris's are required.
An understanding of the Iris is necessary. I have given names to the various shapes. This assists with remembering the sequence.

The hourglass creates the "Falls"
The arrow creates the "Stamens"
The spearhead creates the "Standards"
The wrench creates the centre petals.
The waistcoat creates the "Calyx"

They all work in harmony with each other like a well oiled machine.
The spearhead stands tall while the arrow separates the hourglass from the wrench.

PAINTING: Follow the Step by Step colouring chart on the inside back cover.

NOTE: The underside of each shape is painted after the top has dried.
Character lines are also painted when the petals are dry.

The Hourglass:

1. Colour the centre bright yellow. In the illustration, the dark, vertical section represents the yellow paint.
2. From the top of the waistline of the hourglass downwards, paint soft green.
3. Paint the remainder with Dioxazine Violet including around the edges of the soft green.
   Blend these colours together. Allow to dry.
4. Repeat the steps above on the back of the petals. The back does not have to be as exact. Allow to dry.

Arrow:

5. Paint the stem in soft green.

Wrench:

1. The white circles represent the nodules. Do not paint this section on one side of the shapes.
2. Paint the shapes on both sides with Dioxazine Violet.
3. When completed, paint the nodules very pale with the same colour. Use more water. Touch the nodules with a tissue to remove the excess.

Spearhead: Standard petal.

1. Paint both sides of the shapes with Dioxazine Violet.

Fine Character Line:

Paint the Hourglass and Spearhead with many close,fine character lines. Use the same colour but less water and a Liner/Size 0 paintbrush. The reverse/underneath side does not require character lines. Allow to dry.

Character and composition:

1. The Hourglass has "**half moon**" character lengthwise below the black line.
2. Turn over and give gentle "**outwards curving**" character to the top of the petal only. This petal is the "fall" petal.
3. Glue the stamen into position on each petal.
4. Place the wrench on top of the moulding pad with the nodules facing downwards. With the Shape Mate emboss/rub with a circular motion the nodules only. They will now protrude and the paler shade will be seen when the Iris is completed.
5. The top of the wrench has **"rolling character"**. Hold one tip of the wrench with the closed tweezers/quilling tool and roll backwards on the opposite side to the nodules. Roll firmly towards the dotted section indicated in the diagram.

   The nodules now protrude on the opposite side to the rolling.
6. Adhere this section to the combined hourglass and arrow head. The nodules face the stamen. This completes the "fall" section of the Iris.
7. To the "standard" petals give mild "**halfmoon character**" to the length of the petal.

Bringing the Iris into bloom:

1. Cut a strip of green paper to the size shown in the diagram below. The dots indicate the petals' position, cut the paper straight.
2. Glue the six completed sections/petals in space shown in the following manner. One dot represents the shank/small base stem of one petal. The petals must be between the two white lines. The shanks do not overlap, they are independent of each other.

Enlarged diagram for better viewing.

3. Falls are glued first on numbers 1, 3 and 5.
4. Standards are glued on 2, 4 and six. Allow to dry.
5. Hold the right hand end of the paper, Step 4, with the reversable tweezers. Roll firmly up to the X and glue, do not remove the tweezers. Continue rolling and gently roll over the petals taking care to keep the petals in their correct position. Glue the end to secure and remove the tweezers carefully.

Note: A quilling tool can also be used for this part of the flower. Before gluing, check the section with the petals. The petals just meet when one full turn has been completed. They do not overlap. To adjust, add or remove a small piece of the paper. This is necessary if the paper you are using and/or the tightness of your rolling differs from mine. This is a minor adjustment.

Calyx: Punch one, green waistcoat per flower. Place on the moulding pad and give **"wrap around character"**. Situate the tweezers, from the top, into position near the flap on the right hand side. Place the glue on this flap. With your thumb press the flap on the left, on top of the glued section.

Combine: Add glue to the rolled, bottom section of the completed Iris and adhere inside the calxy.

Leaves: Cut one or two sword like leaves per Iris, shape is shown in diagram.

Broderie Anglaise.

Punches required:  Corner Flower.

Paper: Opaque Parchment/Vellum. A4 sheet, extra for the larger top layer.

Size: The Broderie Anglaise pattern is completed before cutting the Parchment to size.

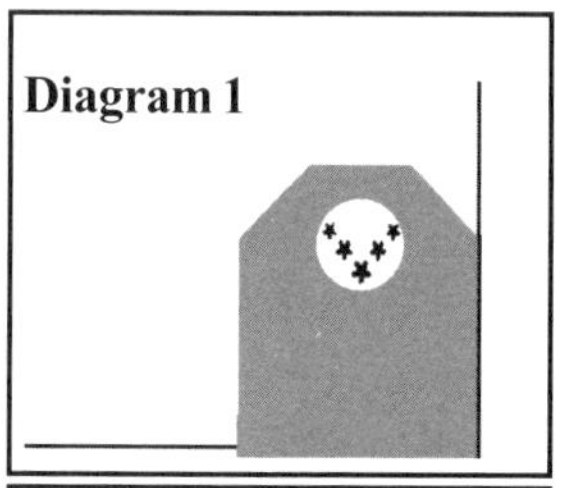

Broderie Anglaise:

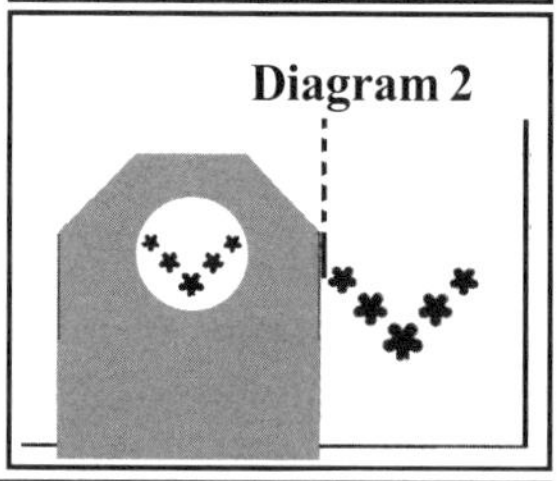

Note: The punched pattern is along the width edge of the paper.

1. The punch is pushed in as far as the paper allows for the first row of punched flowers. Line up the edge of the punch with the right hand, side edge and punch once.
2. Slide the punch along the edge of the paper, line up the side of the punch on the edge of the last flower in the Corner Flower pattern. Diagram 2.
3. Repeat Step 2. Diagram 3.
4. Continue punching until the width of the paper is completed. Remove the punch.
5. Use a set square to draw a line, in white pencil, parallel with the punched edge.

The measurement must be exact, 36mm/1 13/32" high. Diagram 4, black arrow.

Diagram 1

Diagram 2

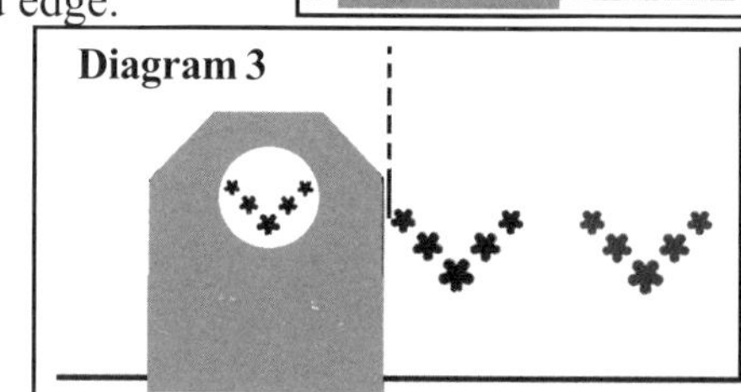
Diagram 3

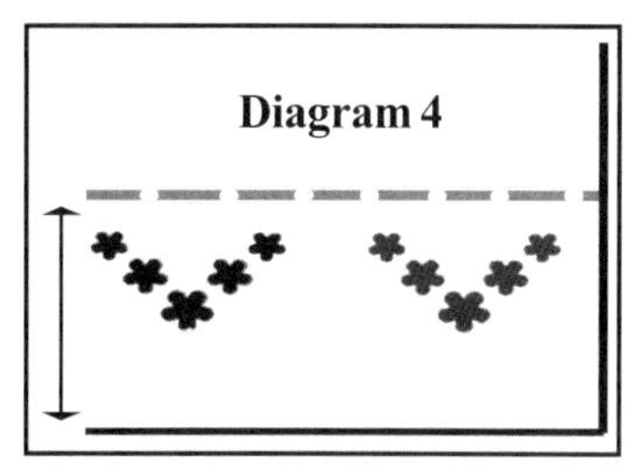
Diagram 4

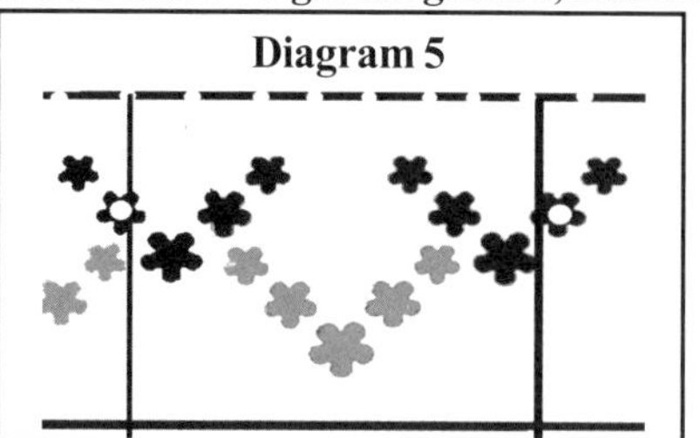
Diagram 5

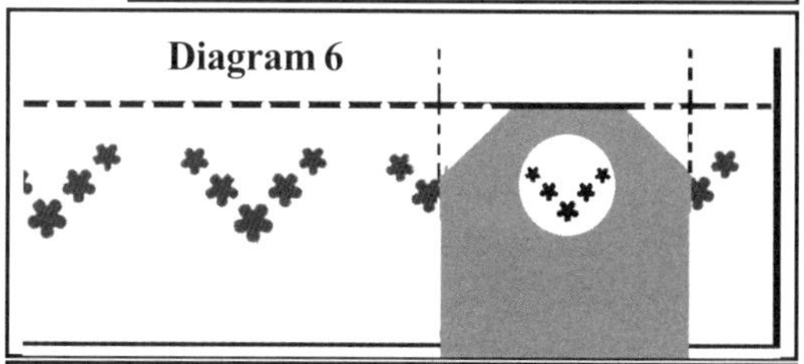

6. Place the punch near the right hand, side edge. Line up both sides of the punch with the flowers previously punched, as seen in diagram 5 above. The flowers are identified with a white circle.
7. Line up the top of the punch with the line drawn in Step 5.
8. Slide the punch along the edge repeating Steps 6 and 7 above.

Note: The Steps are shown in diagrams 6, 7 and 8. The black flowers represent the first row while the grey flowers are now being punched.

9. Complete the edge.

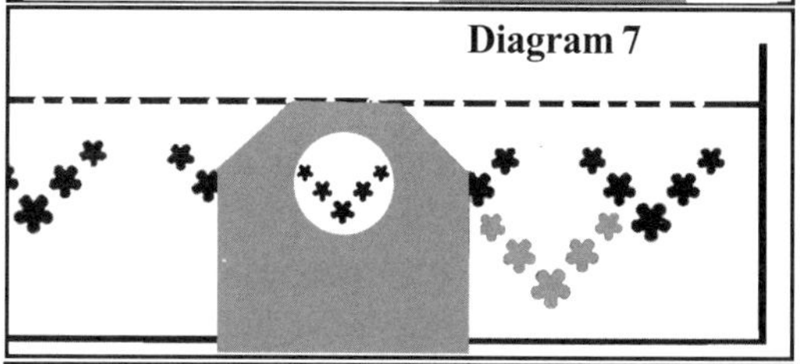

Top layer:

Optional: Diagrams 9, **to scale**, and 10 show a different, top pattern. Choose your design. Diagram 10 requires another piece of parchment.

10. Repeat the flower pattern along the opposite edge for Diagram 9. Use the second piece of parchment for Diagram 10.
11. Both the base and top patterns match.
12. Make an embossing template with the Corner Flower punch. Instructions on page 40.

Diagram 6

Diagram 7

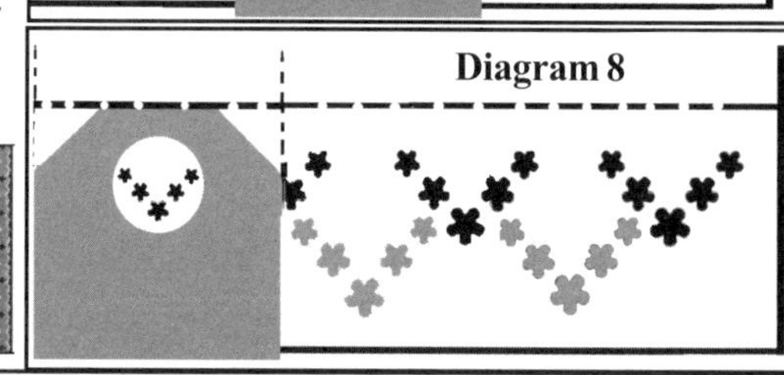
Diagram 8

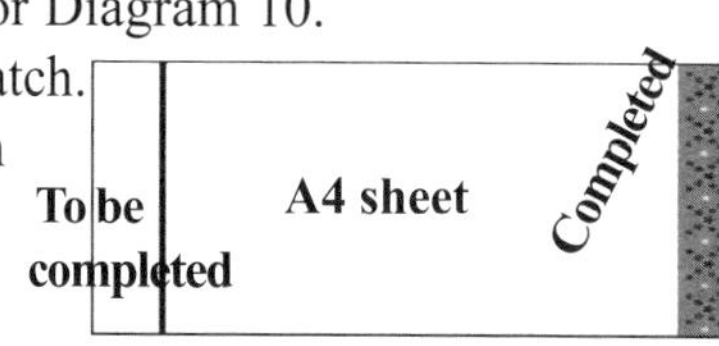

Use the template for the next Step. Embossing the back of the Parchment is achieved on the moulding or embossing pad. A light source is not required.

13. Emboss the tiny flowers as seen in the diagrams.
14. Emboss the tiny dots around the large flowers.
15. Trim both the side edges with Ripple scissors. Emboss the edges twice if necessary.

Continued on page 45.

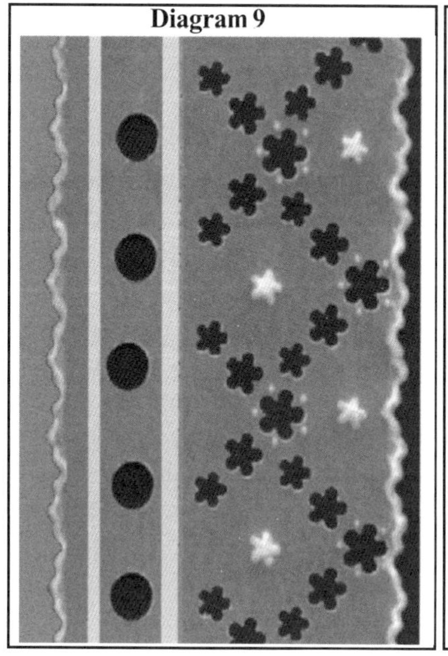
Diagram 9

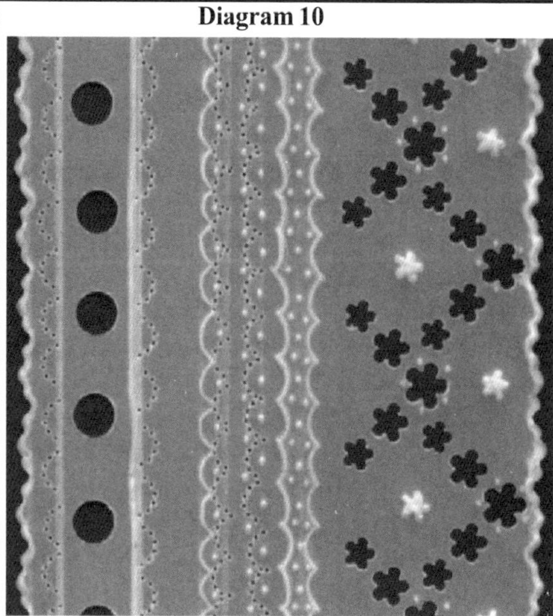
Diagram 10

Broderie Anglaise

Lilacs and Blossoms
for a very
Special Occasion.

A Staircase of Daphne.

Designed
for
Photo Albums
and
Scrapbooking.

A Home for Violets.

Flowers, their names and where to find them.

Name	3D	Flat
Agapanthus	Floral Punch Craft II	
Aluminium Plant, *ground cover*	Floral Punch Craft II	
Banksia	Floral Punch Craft II	
Begonia	Floral Punch Craft	
Boronia	Floral Punch Craft II	
Bottlebrush	Floral Punch Craft II	Floral Punch Craft
Carnations	Floral Punch Craft II	Floral Punch Craft IV
Daffodils	Floral Punch Craft II	Floral Punch Craft IV
Dahlias	Floral Punch Craft II	
Daphne	Floral Punch Craft V	Floral Punch Craft V
Double Impatiens	Floral Punch Craft II	
Flowering Cherry Plum, *Prunis blireiana,*	Floral Punch Craft V	
Flowering Gum	Floral Punch Craft II	
Forget-me-nots	Floral Punch Craft IV	Floral Punch Craft IV
Fuchsia	Floral Punch Craft II	
Freesia		Floral Punch Craft IV
Gypsophilus	Floral Punch Craft II	
Heliconia	Floral Punch Craft IV	
Hydrangea	Floral Punch Craft	
Iris	Floral Punch Craft V	Floral Punch Craft V
Johnny-jump-up		Floral Punch Craft IV
Lilac	Floral Punch Craft V	Floral Punch Craft V
Liliums	Floral Punch Craft V	
Lily of the Valley	Floral Punch Craft	
Lobelia		Floral Punch Craft IV
Maiden Hair Fern	Floral Punch Craft II	
Marguerite Daisies	Floral Punch Craft II	
Marigolds	Floral Punch Craft II	
Pansies	Floral Punch Craft II	Floral Punch Craft IV
Poinsettia	Floral Punch Craft II	Floral Punch Craft IV
Queensland Umbrella Plant	Floral Punch Craft II	
Rose, medium	Floral Punch Craft	
Rose, small	Floral Punch Craft	
Rose, very small	Floral Punch Craft V	
Senecia cruenta, *cineraria*	Floral Punch Craft V	Floral Punch Craft V
Violets	Floral Punch Craft V	Floral Punch Craft V
Water Lily	Floral Punch Craft II	
Wattle	Floral Punch Craft II	

Floral Punch Craft III, is an instructional video showing, in detail, the moulding and shaping techniques of this craft. The flowers were designed especially for the video. This video is readily available from your Floral Punch Craft outlet.

A Home for Violets.

Punches required:

CP-1 Kikyou (M) Large/Jumbo House  Border Frame "Flower"

Paper/cardboard: Blue for the base.
Brown for the tree. Fawn for the fence.
White and red for the houses.
Deep green for the hill. Mid green for mats.

Violets:

The Violets are punched by the CP-1 Kikyou (M) punch. Eleven in all.
Follow the paper colouring and character painting as for the Violets on page 25.

Leaves:

The leaves are punched with the Iris/Violet combination punch.
Only a small part of the leaves is seen due to the size of these Violets.

Tree:

1. Trace the tree. Use the tracing as a template to cut the brown paper/cardboard to the correct shape.
2. Note the light and dark shades of the tree trunk shown in the diagram.
   Where a branch joins the trunk, it throws a shadow below and just above.
   You colour the shadows to give a 3D appearance to a flat object.
3. Colour the tree trunk with water soluble pencils in the following manner to add character.

a. Use two different shades of brown, one bright, the other mid brown and a black pencil.

Use the side of the lead, never the point.

b. Rub the bright brown over trunk. Use the side of the pencil, not the point.
c. Up the centre of the trunk, rub over with the mid brown.
d. On the left hand side, rub near the edge only, with the black pencil.
e. Rub the branches with the bright brown pencil.
f. Rub the centre of the larger branches with the mid brown pencil.
g. Rub the bottom of the branches with the black pencil.
h. Use the black pencil to shade the shadows above and below the branch joins.
i. With a damp paintbrush, paint over the top with water and blend the colours.
j. If more shading is required, when dry, add more colouring to the section and paint with water.

4. When completed, adhere into position with the double sided sticky tape.

Tree Leaves:

Use green water soluble crayon, water and a barely damp sea sponge and sponge in the leaves as seen in the illustration. Test before commencing as a wet sea sponge will not be satisfactory.

Mats:

Cut to size and adhere into position with the double sided sticky tape. Adhere the Violets near the base mat.

House:

1. Punch three white shapes with the large House punch.
2. Punch three red shapes with the same punch.
3. Trim the three red houses to the shape shown.
4. Turn one white house over so the chimney is on the other side. This is the back shape.
5. Adhere a red roof to each of the white houses.
6. Remove from one shape, the chimney and part of the top as seen in garage.
7. Join two houses together.
8. Adhere the garage in place.
9. Add windows and doors cut from scrap pieces of cardboard.

Step 3.

Step 6.

Step 7.

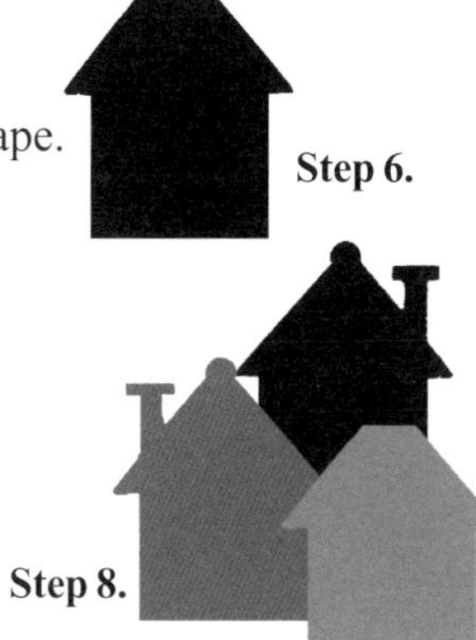

Step 8.

Fence:

1. Punch fawn paper, twice with the Border Frame and trim to length required.
2. Chalk a driveway between the garage and the fence.

REMEMBER: Acid free cardboard is required for the mats and the leaves if touching the photos.

Lilacs and Blossoms for a very Special Occasion.

Punches required:
Silhouette Flower No 1 or Daisy, Medium Four Hearts
Corner Flower and Super Giant Ash Leaf.

Small Impatiens

Mini Flower

Paper: Green for the background.
Green for the trellis and oval.
Dark green for the Ash Leaf shapes. Pale green for the Lilac leaves.
White for the trellis blossoms. Lilac for the Lilac tree.

Trellis:

Diagram 1

Diagram 2

1. From the green paper/cardstock, punch a row of Four Hearts along one edge. Move the punch as far into the edge of the paper as it will allow and line up the edge of the punch with the side edge of the paper. Punch one shape.
2. Slide the punch along the edge and stop when you can see a tiny "V" shape appear in the last heart shape. See diagram 1.
3. Repeat Step 2, continue until the side pattern is complete.
4. See further instruction in detail on page 47.

Note: One side of the trellis is oblong, the other L shaped.
Join the two together to create the complete trellis.
The top of the trellis can be extended for a 12" X 12" scrapbook.

✻ When a single row of the Four Heart punch's trellis is required, a curved arch is made. This allows more space on the base shape. It is particularly pleasant on a greeting card.
When required, the illusion of tendrils is added with the aid of the Mini Swirl punch.

Oval:
1. Trace the oval from the illustration and use it to make a template for the oval shape.
2. Cut the green paper/cardstock to the same size. If paper is used adhere it to a cardboard backing with double sided sticky tape for strength.
3. Adhere onto the page with the same tape when the trellis is in place.

Blossoms:

1. Punch 4 Daisy shapes from white paper. Paint the tips of the daisy shapes in magenta.
2. When dry, cut into eight separate petals. This shape is the blossom for the trellis.
3. Punch with the Ash Leaf, 24 or more shapes to trail in and out of the trellis.

Lilac:
1. Cut the base shapes and the three tiny segments, diagrams on page 46**.** Lilac or white carboard is suitable.
2. Punch out dozens of the Corner Flower shapes from lilac paper and a few Mini Flowers.
3. Adhere the Mini Flowers and some of the Corner Flower shapes to the back base shape. To check if the area to be seen is covered, place the front base shape on top. Continue until complete.
   Note: There is no need to cover the entire back base shape.
4. The front base shape is entirely covered with the shapes from the Corner Flower punch until completed.
5. Trim strips of double sided, sticky mounting tape and adhere behind the front shape.
6. Peel off the backing and adhere the front to the back base shape so the straight base edges appear as one. The thinness of the mounting tape between the base shapes, should not upset the book.

Adding demension:
1. Rub a little lilac watersoluble pencil/crayon onto a small up-side-down lid. Add a touch of water and with a paintbrush, colour, what appears to be the underneath side of the branches with the tinted water. The paint brush is quite damp when tinting to add depth to a flat object.
2. Paint with brown and black pencils/crayons, the trunk and a few tiny branches as seen in the coloured illustration.

Leaves:
1. Punch, in the lighter green, a dozen Small Impatiens leaves.
2. Adhere the whole leaf or trim when necessary, to add a touch of green throughout the Lilac.

Lilac Placement: Adhere the Lilac into the position shown in the illustration.

REMEMBER: Acid free cardboard is required for the mat.

A Staircase of Daphne.

Punches required:

Mini Flower

Mini Star (1)

Corner Flower

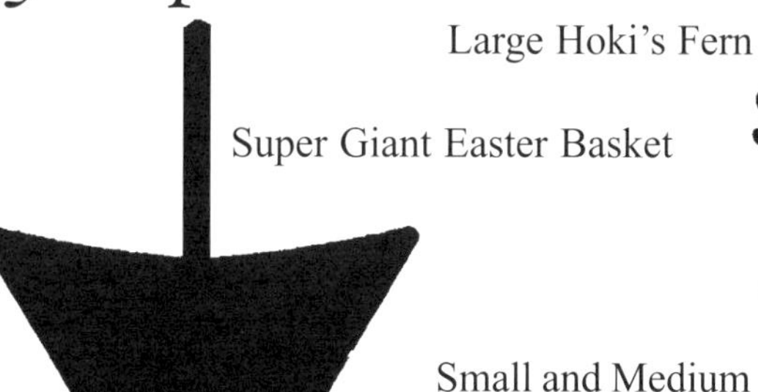
Super Giant Easter Basket

Large Hoki's Fern

Small and Medium Birch Leaves

Paper: Very pale pink for the Daphne.
Two shades of green for the Daphne and fern leaves.
Purple velour.
Base colour is pale pink while the mounts are Heather (Dusty Pink).
Off white, thick, rough textured paper for the steps. This gives the appearance of rendered bricks.

Shapes:

The shapes for the Daphne are punched out after painting the under side.

Staircase:

1. Trace the design from the illustration and use it as a template to cut the textured paper.
2. Adhere into position on the base sheet using double sided sticky tape.

Daphne:

1. Paint a quarter of an A4 sheet, very pale pink paper with water soluble pencils/crayons in a magenta colour.
2. Allow to dry.
3. Using the paper from Step 1 and the Mini Star (1), punch thirty shapes.
4. Punch ten of each shape using the Small and Medium Birch Leaf.
5. Trim the Birch leaves as shown in diagram. Various sizes are required.
6. Glue the stems of three small leaves together on a small scrap of paper.
7. Underneath Step 6, glue two larger leaves in between.
8. Adhere seven or eight Star shapes to the centre.
   Turn a few over to show the magenta underside.
9. Repeat these steps for the second basket.

Baskets:

1. From cardboard, Punch three baskets.
2. Cut two of the baskets as shown in diagram.
   Use the base only for the two baskets on the staircase.
3. Adhere the two basket shapes from Step 2 on the staircase as seen in illustration.
4. Adhere the third basket at the bottom of the staircase, see illustration.

Completing the staircase baskets:

1. Glue a group of leaves/flowers above the top edge of each basket.
2. Add extra leaves where required.
3. Add extra Star shapes peeping out from the extra leaves.
4. With a burgundy, felt tipped pen touch the centre of each Star to show the centre of each shape.

Third Basket:

1. Punch ten Mini Flowers from the purple velour paper.
   Remember, place the paper in the punch with the velour side facing downwards.
2. Punch nine green shapes using the Hoki's Fern.
3. Use the Corner Flower to punch out tiny magenta flowers from the remains of the painted paper above.
4. Adhere into position using the illustration as a guide line.
   The magenta colour is the correct side for the Corner Flower shapes.

Mats:

1. The mats are cut to size from cardboard called Heather/Dusty Pink.
2. Adhere them into position with double sided sticky tape.

REMEMBER: Acid free cardboard is required for the mats and the leaves if touching the photos.

Embossing and Pattern Making with the aid of Craft Punches.

Paper Embossing is sometimes called "dry embossing". You make your own stencils from punches.
Layers of cardboard are required to give the depth. The exact amount will vary according to the thickness of the cardboard.

Daisies

Coloured illustration on page 30.

Paper Embossing requirements:
Light source.
Punch/pattern which is called a template.
Embossing tool.
Paper/cardboard. Masking tape is optional.

Explanations:

* Paper Embossing must have a source of light behind the paper/cardboard.
* Thick or dark paper/cardboard will not allow the light to penetrate, pattern cannot be seen.
* Embossing tool. There are many brands, sizes and prices on the market. The Shape Mate is too large.
* Masking tape holds the pattern and template together when embossing.
* Emboss means "make protuberant".
* Embossing the outline will cause the whole image to move downwards towards the glass.
* Emboss around the outline once. Repeated embossing or outlining creates unwanted lines.
* Embossing the outline then the complete shape of the image will create unwanted lines inside the contour. The advantage is the embossed section will protrude more. Weigh up the benefit against the unwanted lines.

Template:
A template is made from any material with the following requirements:
(a) Correct thickness.
(b) Capacity to be cut.
The template must be placed on the glass. The template is the pattern.

Sound:
Sometimes, the sound changes as the embossing tool moves across the grain of the cardboard. Similar to a finger nail on a blackboard.

Paper Embossing, creating the templates:
Punched templates (cardboard) require several layers of cardboard to give the depth. The exact amount will vary according to the thickness of the cardboard. It is better to use an extra layer than force the punch.

1. Use the Daisy or Silhouette Flower and punch three or four shapes from cardstock.
2. Adhere the layers together with glue or sticky tape.
   The shapes must be exactly on top of each other and give the appearance of one shape only.
3. Repeat the steps above using the Large Oak Leaf and the Small Daisy punches.

Creating the Design:

4. Place the template on top of the card in the position you wish to commence embossing.
5. Hold the template in position with several pieces of masking tape.
6. Turn the card over so the **template** is **touching** the lightbox's **glass** or substitute.
   When using a lightbox, turn the power on only when embossing to prevent heating the glass.
7. Run the ball of the embossing tool around the top, inside edge of the outline. Keep a smooth running line with the embossing ball. Repeat with a large ball, if required.
   Note: Care should be taken not to slip off the edge of the pattern when embossing. This is usually caused by going too fast. Slow down. Repeated embossing backwards and forwards creates unwanted lines.
8. Continue, using the other templates, until the design is complete.

Adding colour:

9. Use water soluble crayons to paint the raised area called embossing. This is not always required.

Border: Border Decoration punch, No.106. The coloured illustration is on page 30.

1. Make the template following the instructions above.
2. Leave the base strip intact. The scallops are used to emboss the edge of the card.
3. The white line in diagram 1 shows the position of the punch, when sliding the punch along the edge, to punch the second pattern. There are seven tiny holes, overlap the seventh hole when punching the next pattern.

Diagram 1

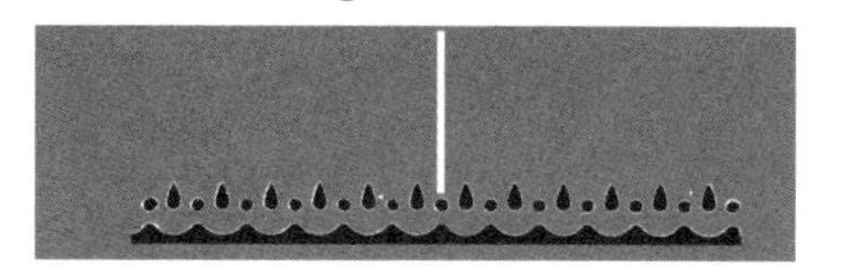

Diagram 2. Four sets of punched shapes, overlapping on the seventh hole.

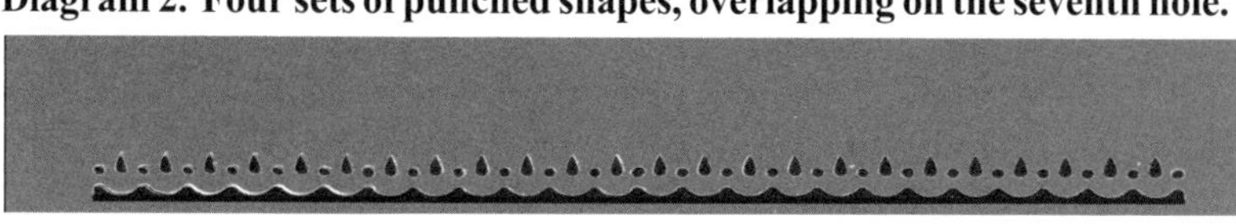

Embossing and Pattern Making with the aid of Craft Punches continued.

Punches required: Hearts.

Hearts of Love.

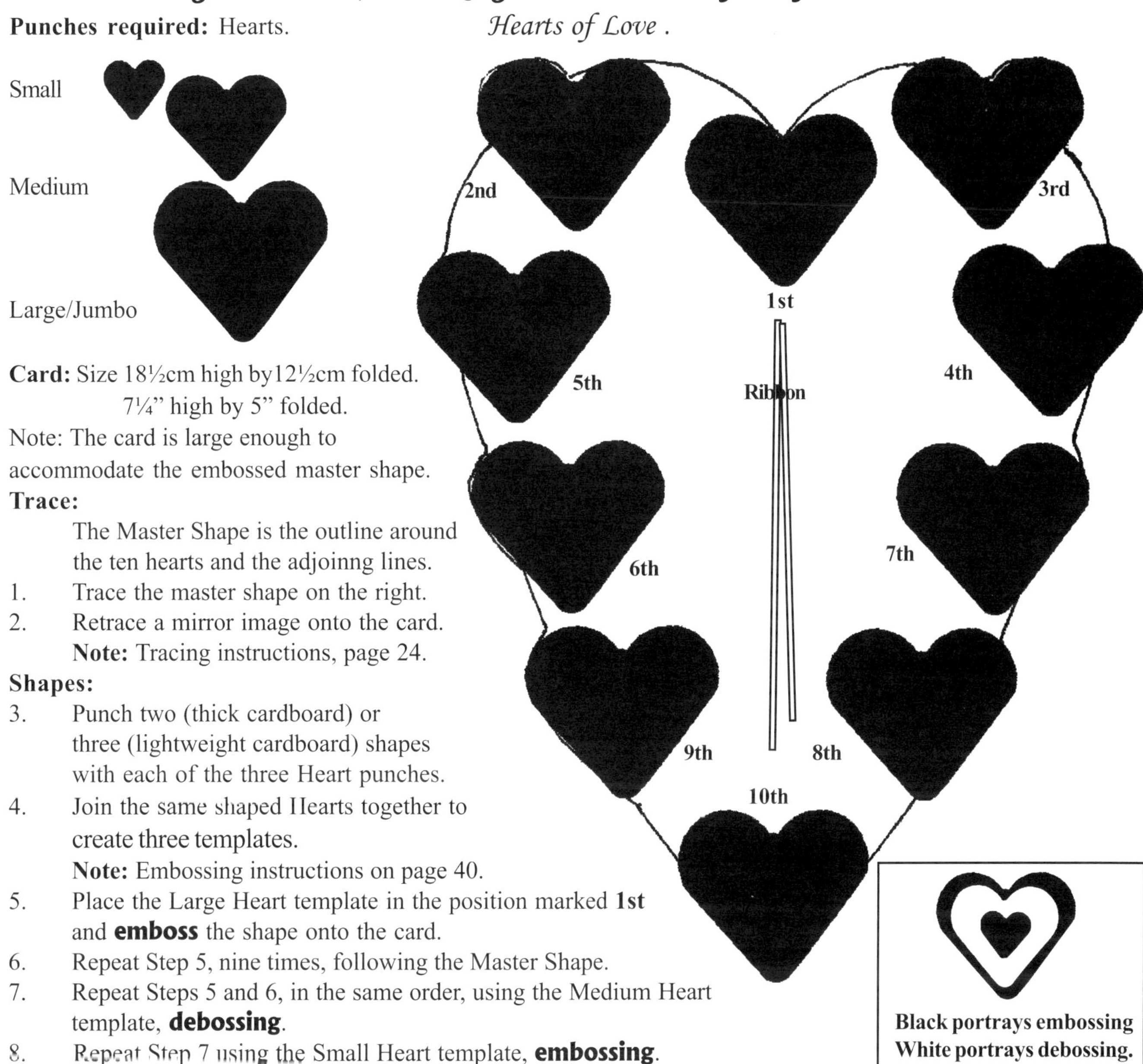

Card: Size 18½cm high by12½cm folded.
7¼" high by 5" folded.

Note: The card is large enough to accommodate the embossed master shape.

Trace:

The Master Shape is the outline around the ten hearts and the adjoinng lines.

1. Trace the master shape on the right.
2. Retrace a mirror image onto the card.
   Note: Tracing instructions, page 24.

Shapes:

3. Punch two (thick cardboard) or three (lightweight cardboard) shapes with each of the three Heart punches.
4. Join the same shaped Hearts together to create three templates.
   Note: Embossing instructions on page 40.
5. Place the Large Heart template in the position marked **1st** and **emboss** the shape onto the card.
6. Repeat Step 5, nine times, following the Master Shape.
7. Repeat Steps 5 and 6, in the same order, using the Medium Heart template, **debossing**.
8. Repeat Step 7 using the Small Heart template, **embossing**.

Ribbons:

9. Stamp the greeting onto cardboard, the same colour and texture as above. The words are stamped apart.
10. Place the Medium Heart template over each word, in turn and emboss. Repeat using the large Heart.
11. Cut around the outside of the Large Heart shapes. Note, there is no debossing.
12. Fold a length, 15.5cm/6", of ribbon and off set the ends. Adhere to the card between the two centre Hearts as shown. Adhere Step 11 to the ribbons and a complimentary coloured insert.

Hints.

1. During hot weather P.V.A. glue thickens. Add a few drops of water to the glue and stir with a toothpick.
2. P.V.A. glue dries clear but shiny. A small amount only is required.
   Too much glue will stiffen the paper when it dries. Character, such as curving, cannot be achieved to your advantage due to this stiffness.
   The more you use the wetter the paper becomes. This in turn weakens the paper and tearing may occur. Excess glue takes too long to dry and gives you no advantage.
3. Keep the points of your tweezers "**glue free**" by occasionally dipping them in cold water and wiping dry with a tissue. Repeat as necessary.
4. Use plenty of water when tinting or colouring. Start with a light tint and if required add extra colouring. It is easier to be too light, then add extra, than too dark and need to remove the colouring.
5. If water soluble paint is applied too dark, wash over with a damp paint brush and dab with a soft tissue.
6. If a shade of paper is unavailable, colour your own.

Senecia, cineraria 3D.

Punches required: Silhouette Flower or Daisy — Mini Flower — Medium Maple

Optional: Bow

Paper: White paper for the Cinerarias.
Black velour paper for the centres.
Green for the leaves.

Painting: Use water soluble pencils/crayons.

Diagram 1

Flowers:

1. Punch two Daisy flowers to create one Cineraria.
2. Paint the ends of the petals in a suitable Cineraria colour. See below.
3. When dry, cut the petals into eight separate petals as shown in diagram 2.
4. Cut a strip, 4.5mm/3/16" wide by the full length of an A4 sheet of paper.
5. Cut a green stem, (double thickness, glued together) 6cm/2 ¾" in length and in width 2mm/1/8'. Adhere it near the right hand end, diagram 3.
6. Roll Step 4, with the closed tweezers, into a tight coil. Adhere the end to secure it.
7. Gently remove the tweezers and insert one prong only inside the centre of the coil, the other on the outside.
8. Cut a strip of white or green paper to the **exact** length and width shown in diagram 4 below.

Diagram 2

Diagram 3

Diagram 4, base strip

9. Mark the two white lines seen on the base strip.
10. Glue twelve to fourteen petals between the two white lines. Commence from the white line on the left hand side. Each petal overlaps but not the points.

Note: The points are glued near the top of the base strip.
The base points do not overlap, each petal is independant of the other.
Diagram 5 is for viewing the placement of the petals. The black and white sections are petals, six are shown.

Diagram 5

11. Place a few small dabs of glue along the base strip. Glue the right hand end to the coil the tweezers are holding. Roll the tweezers in a circle and adhere the base strip.
12. Attach the end of the base strip to the completed, tight coil and open the petals outwards.
13. Punch one Mini Flower shape for each flower from the black velour paper. Turn the paper to the reverse side before punching.
14. Place on the moulding pad and give "**beehive character**" with the Shape Mate from the reverse side.
15. Glue the beehived shape to the centre of the flower.

Leaves:

16. Punch one green leaf for each two flowers.
17. Trim to the shape shown and vein on the moulding pad.
18. Add a stem to each leaf.

Displaying: Gather the stems together and display the arrangement as a bouquet.

Senecia shadings come in a multitude of colours. Dusty Miller is one of the Senecia varieties. Cineraria is the variety being created here. Really, only one colour should be used for a display of the size shown in the coloured illustration. I have used three different colours to show a selection. The flat Cinerarias in the tub, near the fence, are a true indication of how they grow.
Note: There is variation between individuals when rolling with the closed tweezers/quilling tool, and also, the type of paper used, the spare petals are to fill in any gaps that appear after rolling is completed.

Senecia, cineraria - flat.

Punches required: Small Daisy Small Maple Corner Flower

Paper:

White and three shades of green plus suitable cardstock for the tub.
The grass is green Hemp paper.

Display:

1. Punch two white shapes per flower and paint the tips as for the 3D above. Allow to dry.
2. Glue one on top of the other and off centre the tips.
3. Trim the Small Maple leaf as seen in diagram.
4. Punch one vase shape and trim to create a tub.

Senecia, cineraria - flat continue.

5. Use chalk and shade the sides of the tub darker. This gives the vase a 3D appearance.
6. Fill the tub with the flowers. Where required, cut in half, as seen in illustration.
7. Complete with the leaves.

Watering Can:

1. Punch the shape in Copper. Turn the shape over and place on the pad.
2. Tap the shape with a large embossing tool similar to hammering a nail head.
3. Turn the shape over to the front.

Trees:

1. Punch four, green trees. Two in pale green for the shrubs.
   One tree is seen on the left hand side. The second, on the far side of the hill, on the right, just peeping over the top. Trim the tree to size.
   Shrubs:
2. Remove the trunk from the two, pale green trees.
3. For 3D effect, use chalks. Darker on the left and underneath plus the shadow behing the front shrub.
4. Adhere a piece of sticky mounting tape behind the front shrub.

Fence:

1. Punch the fence, from soft white cardstock, using the Film Strip punch.

* The Film Strip removes seven rectangular shapes.
* One of these shapes overlaps giving six shapes plus the overlaping shape. Example: Punch twice to make thirteen rectangles.
* The black dot in the diagram indicates the punched shape that lines up the Film Strip to create the fence.

   Fence base:
2. Insert the paper, line up the side of the punch with the side edge of the paper.
3. Punch and slide is the action.
   Punch the paper and slide the punch along the edge until it overlaps the last punched rectangle.
4. Repeat Step 3 three times.
   Fence top:
5. To allow the punch to come close to the previously punched shapes, without touching them, trim the width of the paper to 24mm/15/16".
   Repeat Step 3, along the trimmed edge, four times. Line up the missing rectangles from Step 3 before commencing. The result is the fence rail. Remove the excess paper
6. Trim the shapes to resemble pickets.
   Gate:
7. The gate requires the width of four pickets.
8. Remove the tops from the two outer pickets. Add a small piece of cardboard to extend the height. Trim the tops of the extentions into pickets.
   Adhere two, slim strips of cardboard, at the back of the two centre pickets

Assembling the shapes: *Check the coloured illustration as a placement guide line.*

1. Trace the green hills and use the tracing as a template. The base of the hills stops behind the bottom rail of the fence, when in position.
2. Cut the hills to the traced shapes. Use the lighter green for the hill in the background.
3. Trim a piece of green Hemp paper, to meet the base of the hills, behind the bottom rail.
4. Adhere the above into position using double sided sticky tape, followed by the fence.

5. Follow Step 4 with the tub of Cinerarias and the back shrub.
   Trim the right hand edge of the shrub straight as it overlaps the edge of the card.
6. Adhere the Watering Can with silcone glue.
7. Peel the backing off the double sided sticky tape on the back of the second shrub.
8. Place into position along the base of the card, in front of the first shrub.

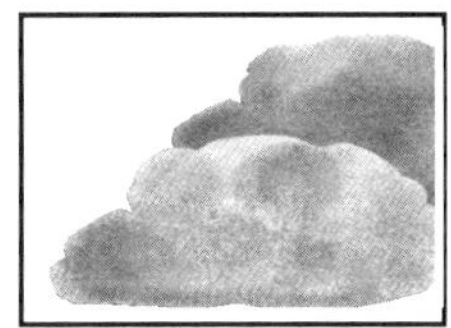

Misty Blooms with Stencilling.

Stencilling is colouring a surface through a hole or image. I recommend a clear lightweight mylar. This is not always available and a good substitute is a piece of acetate similar to a lid of a shirt box/chocolates. I use acetate that I have collected from various sources. The non brittle type.

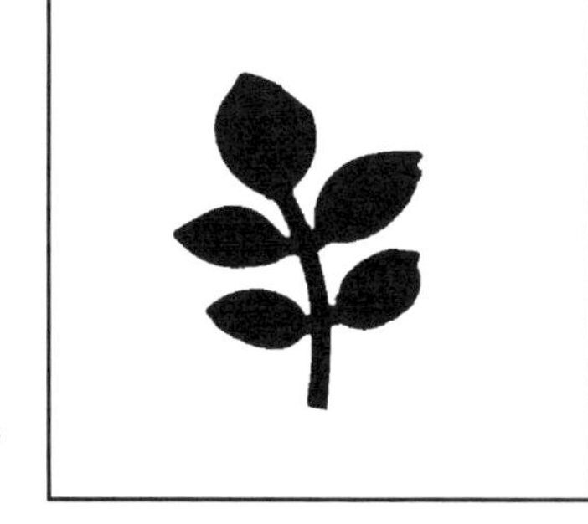

Creating and using a stencil:

1. Cut three pieces of 10cm/4" square acetate.
   The acetate does not have to be a perfect square, the extra size protects the surface/card below.
2. Punch one shape from each square. Use the Large Ash Leaf, Small and Mini Flower punches. Ash Leaf is illustrated.
3. Rub the end of a water soluble crayon around the edge of the punched shapes. Green for leaves and deep and mid orange are shown in the coloured illustration on page 30.
4. The first two diagrams show clean stencils while the third and fourth have crayon on the surface, around the shape.
   Place the dauber on your finger and dampen the sponge end **lightly**. I use the middle finger and test the dauber on a tissue for dampness.
   Check before commencing, too wet and the moisture will run under the stencil.

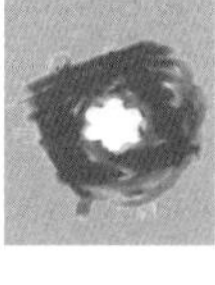

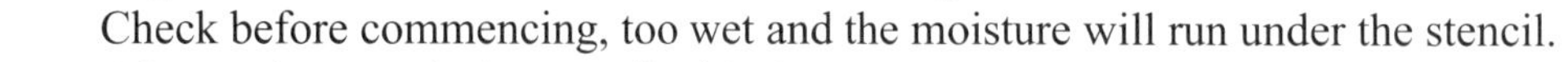

Note: After each use, rub the stencil with the crayon again, if required.
When a little more water is needed, dip a finger in the water and then touch the dauber's sponge.

5. Place the coloured stencil in the starting position on the card and hold with your other hand.
6. With the dauber, wipe across the coloured section into the punched opening .
7. Repeat steps 4 and 5 until the design has been completed.

The coloured illustration is on page 30. For the flowers, I use theSmall and Mini Flower punches to create the stencils. On top of the completed small flower shapes, I placed the mini flower stencil and coloured with a deeper shade of orange using the stencilling method. This gives a deeper shading to the centre of the flowers.

Mermaid

Punches required:
Mini/Baby Drop, Small Egg, Border Decoration No. 101, Medium Balloon and Birch Leaf.

Fold the Balloon in half and trim as shown above, on the left.
The face is a Small Egg shape with the base trimmed to shorten the chin line. Adhere the face behind the hair and add four tiny swirls from the Border punch as seen in illustration. Draw the closed eyes, nostrils and mouth.

Trace and cut, from white cardboard, a base shape slightly smaller than the mermaid above. Cut, from skin tone paper, the exact shape of the mermaid. Adhere to the white base. Punch, from Celestial vellum paper, thirty two Drops and two Birch Leaves. Adhere the leaves to the end of the tail, then the overlapping Drop shapes. Punch and glue into position, two Drops for the bust line and add a strap. Cut an extra right arm and glue on top of the first. Adhere the face into position. The Dolphin is the cut-out from a card.

Heat Embossing *"Butterflies and Bows".*

Butterflies:

1. The butterfly shapes are from the Butterfly Frame Punch. Punch the shapes along the edge of a soft A4 sheet of cardboard. Lengthwise will give you eight butterflies. Cut into a strip for easy handling.
   A Butterfly strip is shown in diagram 1 below.

The strip here shows the position of the Frame Punch to allow eight butterflies to be punched along the length of an A4 sheet of soft cardboard.
The dotted line indicates the position to place the punch.

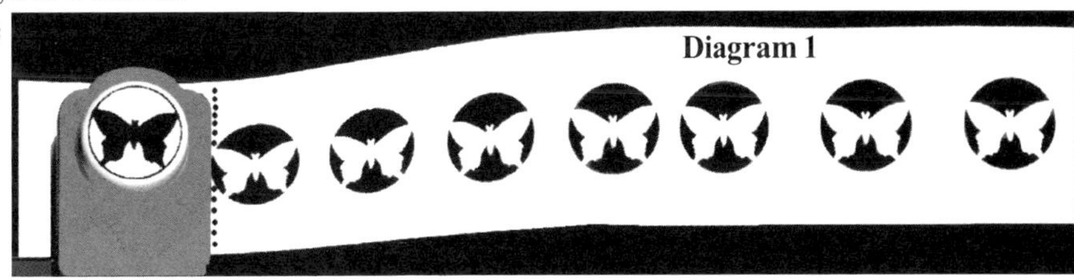
Diagram 1

2. With felt brush markers, colour the butterflies in many shades. Mark in extra character for variation.
3. Place the strip on a waxed piece of paper.
4. Fold a piece of spare paper lengthwise and re-open.
5. Quickly move along the strip of shapes from the palest to the deepest colour with the glue stick.
6. Place on top of Step 4. Sprinkle the shapes with Iridescent Embossing Powder. Shake excess powder onto the spare sheet of paper. Replace the excess powder into its container.
7. Any colour embossing powder can be used, iridescent or clear is used when you wish to see the colour/ pattern underneath. In the coloured illustration iridescent embossing powder is used.
8. Heat the butterflies, face up, over a toaster, to melt the Embossing Powder giving an iridescent effect.
   An Embossing Heat Gun is an advantage but not a necessity.
9. Allow to cool. Remove the butterflies from the frame with scissors and glue into position as required.
   Glue only the body section if the wings are going to be raised.
   For a double butterfly, use two shapes of the same colour. Glue the first flat with PVA glue. For the second, place the glue under the body only. Position it on top of the first body and allow to dry. Craft glue/silicone is necessary as the PVA glue will not hold on top of the embossing.

Bows:

Repeat the above Butterfly steps using the Frame Bow punch.

Frame punches make embossing easy as the shapes do not move around, the frame contains them.

Birds:

1. Turn the Medium Heart Punch over.
2. Insert a piece of black paper into the Punch opening and stop, just below the dip at the top of the heart shape.
3. Punch out the shape seen in diagram 2.
4. Punch another shape in the same manner so as to remove only the top of the heart.
5. Diagram No 3 shows the finished products in the shape of birds in the distance.
6. The small bird was made from a Small Heart Punch.

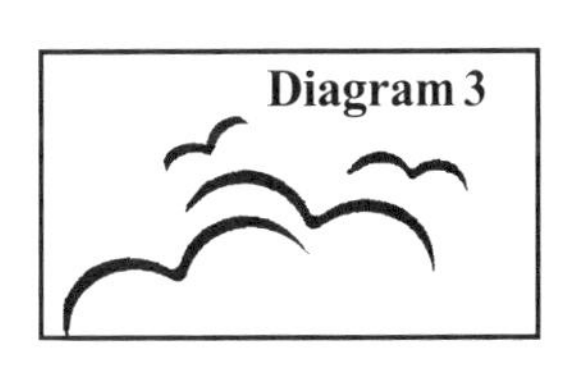
Diagram 3

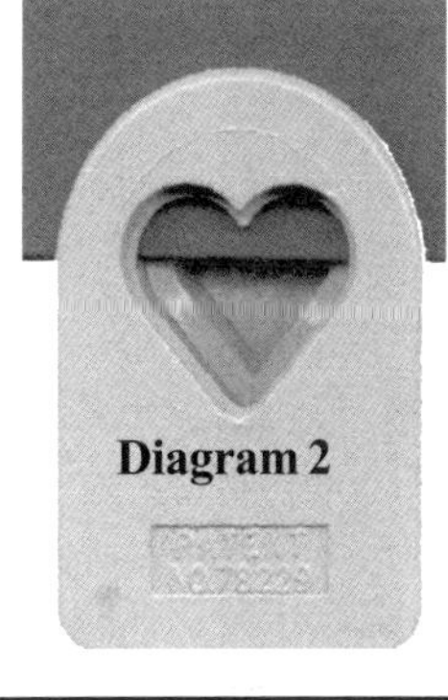
Diagram 2

Broderie Anglaise continued:

For Diagram 10 only: Follow the pattern shown in the diagram with Deet or a Parchment tool.

16. Emboss the two, vertical lines on the pad.
17. Cut the width of the pattern to the exact size shown in diagrams 9 or 10. Place on top of the base pattern.
18. Align the patterns on top of each other. Trim the height of the card to 19cm/7½" and the width to 21cm/8¼".
19. Etch, lightly, the centre line and fold the parchment to form the card.
20. With a Circle punch, remove the holes for the ribbon from the top layer.
21. Thread a white ribbon through the holes.
22. Adhere double sided sticky tape behind the ribbon section, the full length of the design. Pull both ends of the ribbons firmly to remove any slackness before securing with the sticky tape.
23. Remove the sticky tape's backing and adhere onto the base design.
    The combination appears to be a double layer of Broderie Anglaise.
24. Adhere the lemon insert in place to complete the card.

Borders.

Daphne, Border Punch 101.

1. Punch the border along the edge of the cardboard before cutting the card.
2. Place punch along the side edge level with the top edge. PUNCH one pattern.
3. Slide the punch along the edge and line up the right, side edge of the punch with the third last hole in the pattern. PUNCH.
4. Slide the punch along and line up with the third last hole again. PUNCH.
5. Repeat the action until the side edge is completed.
6. Trim the card to size, 19.2cm high by 26.4cm wide, folded 13.2cm.

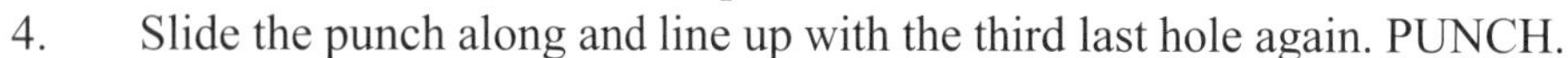

Arch and sides for
"A Basket of Violets".
Diagram is exact.

Take all measurements from the illustration.
Trace the arch and use as a template to reproduce the design.
The sides are cut separately and joined to the arch.

Trellis and Backings for Lilacs, flat:
Take note of the position of the punch. It is always the tip of a heart that acts as a guide line for the punch.
Optional: After punching the first row, draw guide lines as seen below. The diagram below is exact.
Punch one row without trimming the edges. Trim the width of the paper/cardstock to the size below before punching the second row for the trellis. The length depends on the page size.
When punching the top of the trellis, punch along the top from the outside.

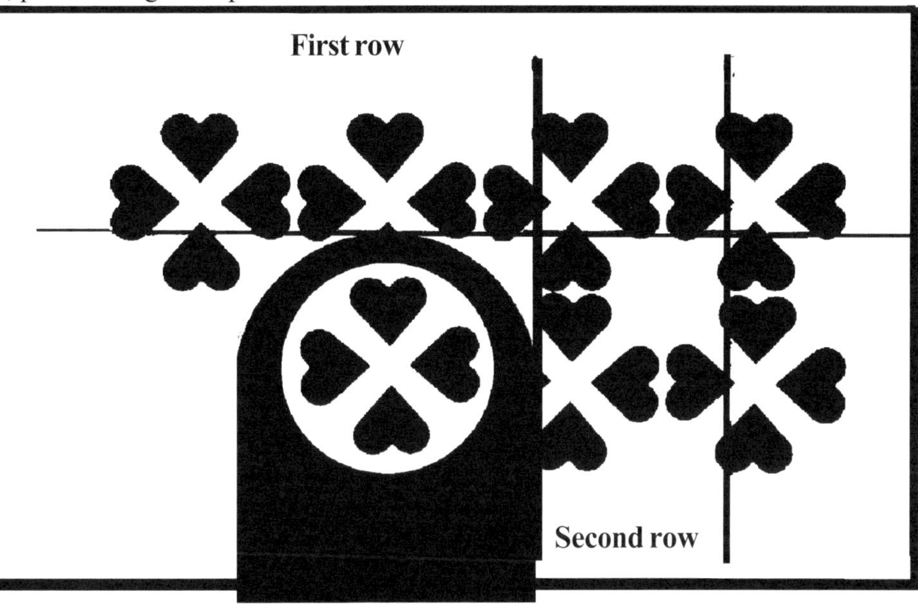

Diagram below shows the L shape for the trellis.

Design for the top of the *Lilac's* card.
This is adhered into position with double sided sticky tape before the Lilac is glued into position.

Lilac 3D ... Section B.
The outline on this oblong is to the exact measurement for the top of the design. Take all measurements from here.

This design shows the two sections combined. Section "A" is the base. Section "B" is adhered on top of the base section. The combination is adhered to the Lilac's base card.

Lilac, 3D ... Section A.

The outline on this oblong is the exact measurement for the base of the design. Take all measurements from here.

Outline the edges in gold.
Use a gold pen and ruler.

Daphne

Punches required: Super Giant Daphne and Lilac combination punch.
Border Decoration Punch No.105.
Paper: Very pale pink for flower, green for leaves and pale green for new growth.
Insert: Sheet of A4, Juni Purple. Cut to size.
Cardboard: Soft Amethyst. The border must be completed before cutting the card to size. Instructions on page 46.
When completed the height is 19.2cm/7 ½" and the width folded, is 13.2cm/5 3/8".
Paint: Magenta water colour.
Gloss: Gloss to paint the leaves. Daphne leaves are glossy.
Twig: From your garden to which the flowers and leaves are adhered.

Shapes: The number of shapes vary due to the size of the flowerettes.
The guide line is: Twenty to twenty-two shapes for a large flowerette.
Fifteen shapes for medium.
Eleven for small.
Bud, six to seven.

Before punching shapes:

1. Paint one side only with the Magenta paint and allow to dry.
   Repeat if the colour is too pale for the outside of the Daphne flower. Allow to dry.

Leaves:

2. Punch six large, green leaves for each flowerette.
3. Place on the moulding pad and give a centre vein to each leaf.
4. Remove and paint with the clear gloss paint. Allow to dry.
5. Adhere three leaves to the tiny circle.
6. Trim 3mm/1/8" off the base of the next three leaves and adhere in between the previous leaves.
7. Punch three small leaves for a new growth section. Repeat Steps 3, 4 and 5 with these leaves.
8. Adhere together, two small strips of pale green paper to the size shown and trim the top to form a point.
9. At the base line only, glue the combined strip on top of one of the small leaves. → →
10. Place the combined shape on the moulding pad and give **"severe cup character"** to the centre of the shape only.
11. Hold the leaves and squeeze, with your fingers, the base of Step 10 to close the shape. This gives the leaves a new growth appearance. The larger leaves can also be utilized.

Flower:

12. Punch out the flower shapes. More can be punched later, if required.
    The white circle indicates the position of the tweezers.
13. Place on top of the moulding pad.
14. Give **"wrap around character"** to all the flower shapes. See page 7.
15. Pick up one shape at a time with the straight or closed tweezers in the position shown in the diagram.
16. Place a touch of PVA glue to the flap indicated by the small circles in the diagram.

16 Roll the shape into a tiny, cone shaped flower.
18. With your left thumb push the flap down to adhere to the other side.

19. Glue extra shapes around a centre flower shape, quantities above.
    Move in a circle, gluing the side of each to another flower.

20. Adhere each flowerette to a group of leaves from above.

Note:
Keep the base points together.

To complete:

21. Adhere the insert inside the folded card with the punched border.
22. Glue the twig into position with PVA glue and allow to dry.
23. Follow the coloured illustration for the placement of the flowers and leaves.

Sand the back of the twig to allow it to sit flat on the card to avoid the card twisting at a later date.